Children's Internet Search:

Using Roles to Understand Children's Search Behavior

Synthesis Lectures on Information Concepts, Retrieval, and Services

Editor
Gary Marchionini, *Affiliation*

Synthesis Lectures on Information Concepts, Retrieval, and Services is edited by Gary Marchionini of the University of North Carolina. The series will publish 50- to 100-page publications on topics pertaining to information science and applications of technology to information discovery, production, distribution, and management. The scope will largely follow the purview of premier information and computer science conferences, such as ASIST, ACM SIGIR, ACM/IEEE JCDL, and ACM CIKM. Potential topics include, but not are limited to: data models, indexing theory and algorithms, classification, information architecture, information economics, privacy and identity, scholarly communication, bibliometrics and webometrics, personal information management, human information behavior, digital libraries, archives and preservation, cultural informatics, information retrieval evaluation, data fusion, relevance feedback, recommendation systems, question answering, natural language processing for retrieval, text summarization, multimedia retrieval, multilingual retrieval, and exploratory search.

Children's Internet Search: Using Roles to Understand Children's Search Behavior
Elizabeth Foss and Allison Druin
September 2014

Digital Library Technologies: Complex Objects, Annotation, Ontologies, Classification, Extraction, and Security
Edward A. Fox, Ricardo da Silva Torres
March 2014

Digital Libraries Applications: CBIR, Education, Social Networks, eScience/Simulation, and GIS
Edward A. Fox, Jonathan P. Leidig
March 2014

Information and Human Values
Kenneth R. Fleischmann
November 2013

Information Retrieval Evaluation
Donna Harman
May 2011

Knowledge Management (KM) Processes in Organizations: Theoretical Foundations and Practice
Claire R. McInerney, Michael E. D. Koenig
January 2011

Search-Based Applications: At the Confluence of Search and Database Technologies
Gregory Grefenstette, Laura Wilber
2010

Information Concepts: From Books to Cyberspace Identities
Gary Marchionini
2010

Estimating the Query Difficulty for Information Retrieval
David Carmel, Elad Yom-Tov
2010

iRODS Primer: Integrated Rule-Oriented Data System
Arcot Rajasekar, Reagan Moore, Chien-Yi Hou, Christopher A. Lee, Richard Marciano, Antoine de Torcy, Michael Wan, Wayne Schroeder, Sheau-Yen Chen, Lucas Gilbert, Paul Tooby, Bing Zhu
2010

Collaborative Web Search: Who, What, Where, When, and Why
Meredith Ringel Morris, Jaime Teevan
2009

Multimedia Information Retrieval
Stefan Rüger
2009

Online Multiplayer Games
William Sims Bainbridge
2009

Information Architecture: The Design and Integration of Information Spaces
Wei Ding, Xia Lin
2009

Children's Interet Search: Using Roles to Understand Children's Search
Behavior Elizabeth Foss and Allison Druin

ISBN: 978-3-031-01158-0 print
ISBN: 978-3-031-02286-9 ebook

DOI 10.1007/978-3-031-02286-9

A Publication in the Springer series
SYNTHESIS LECTURES ON INFORMATION CONCEPTS, RETRIEVAL, AND SERVICES #34
Series Editor: Gary Marchionini, University of North Carolina, Chapel Hill

Series ISSN   1947-945X Print   1947-9468 Electronic

Children's Internet Search:
Using Roles to Understand Children's Search Behavior

Elizabeth Foss and Allison Druin

College of Information Studies, Human-Computer Interaction Lab, University of Maryland, College Park, Maryland

SYNTHESIS LECTURES ON INFORMATION CONCEPTS, RETRIEVAL, AND SERVICES #34

ABSTRACT

Searching the Internet and the ability to competently use search engines are increasingly becoming an important part of children's daily lives. Whether mobile or at home, children use search interfaces to explore personal interests, complete academic assignments, and have social interaction. However, engaging with search also means engaging with an ever-changing and evolving search landscape. There are continual software updates, multiple devices used to search (e.g., phones, tablets), an increasing use of social media, and constantly updated Internet content. For young searchers, this can require infinite adaptability or mean being hopelessly confused.

This book offers a perspective centered on children's search experiences as a whole instead of thinking of search as a process with separate and potentially problematic steps. Reading the prior literature with a child-centered view of search reveals that children have been remarkably consistent over time as searchers, displaying the same search strategies regardless of the landscape of search. However, no research has synthesized these consistent patterns in children's search across the literature, and only recently have these patterns been uncovered as distinct search roles, or searcher types. Based on a four-year longitudinal study on children's search experiences, this book weaves together the disparate evidence in the literature through the use of 9 search roles for children ages 7–15. The search role framework has a distinct advantage because it encourages adult stakeholders to design children's search tools to support and educate children at their existing levels of search strength and deficit, rather than expecting children to adapt to a transient search landscape.

KEYWORDS

information retrieval, internet search, children

Contents

Introduction

Harvey, age 9, sits in front of his mother's MacBook laptop at the dinner table in his family's dining room (see Figure I.1). He's excited, talking about the cable company repair technician who visited his home a few days prior to fix an unstable Internet connection. Harvey's mother stands at the opposite end of the table, alternately ironing dress shirts and chatting with the two researchers who have come to interview Harvey and his 7-year-old brother Jay about their Internet searching. The researchers finish setting up their video camera and turn it on, capturing Harvey, his surroundings, and his computer screen, and after confirming with Harvey that he is ready, they begin his interview.

Figure I.1: Harvey at age 9 (left) and at age 12 (right).

While one researcher takes notes, the other asks Harvey about his Internet search habits and preferences. When Harvey is asked to freely explore the Internet to demonstrate what he usually does when searching, he cheerfully types [delorean pictures]. He clicks on *Google Images*, and finding a picture he likes, he announces, "Ta-da!" as he clicks on the image link. Instead of the expected enlarged image, Harvey is directed to a website filled with ads. When Harvey clicks the browser's back button to navigate away from the undesirable site, a robotic male voice merrily reports, "Congratulations, you won!" Harvey laughs in response, genuinely delighted by this diversion.

A closer examination of Harvey's search for DeLorean car pictures reveals much about his Internet search skills and preferences. Harvey is clearly familiar with keyboarding, using two hands and nearly correct finger positioning. However, he's fairly slow to type, taking almost 20 s to enter his query while visually confirming each key before pressing. The query Harvey enters is correctly spelled, although he doesn't bother with capitalization. Harvey has obviously searched for images before, as he is able to shift between Google's Web results and Image results without hesitation. He is also able to quickly recognize the ad as irrelevant to his query, and knows how to navigate within the browser to return to his search results. Harvey's engagement with the search is notable. He laughs, jokes, and happily demonstrates his search habits as he explores the content he finds.

THE IMPORTANCE OF SEARCH LITERACY

The proliferation of technology in children's lives can be seen in their homes, schools, libraries, museums, and play spaces. These technologies are complementary to children's natural curiosity and desire for play and exploration experiences. Children themselves have recognized this, and are incorporating Internet use into their daily lives at unparalleled rates (Livingstone et al., 2011). Even in children's everyday conversations, a question might arise and they will quickly pull out a computing device to search for answers. If they are not doing this, they may be engaging with game websites in their free time or reaching out to friends via text or Skype to solve difficult homework problems. Even for seemingly trivial and pleasurable engagement, benefits of the Internet span gaining expertise with technology, improving the potential for future employment, educational achievement, and access to educational resources (Davies, 2011; Hannaford, 2012: Jackson et al., 2006; Livingstone and Bober, 2006).

Children and adolescents have information needs that differ from those of adults (Hughes-Hassell and Agosto, 2007). In the past, reliance on peers, mentors, family, teachers, and librarians was common practice for children (Hughes-Hassell and Agosto, 2007), but more recently, the Internet provides a readily available resource for meeting those needs. With laptops, mobile phones, tablets, Wi-Fi, and 4G as common as teddy bears and picture books, so too is searching for information on the Internet (Goldman et al., 2012). The physical space a young searcher occupies and the reason behind initiating a search can have dramatic impacts on search behavior. In the school environment, children often search on imposed topics to satisfy needs originating from an assignment (e.g., Gross, 2006). In other contexts, such as the home setting, children have more computer time, access to broader content, and the freedom to search on subjects of more personal interest (Livingstone and Helsper, 2008; Rideout et al., 2010; Selwyn et al., 2009).

There is much discussion in the research literature regarding information literacies. As described by the American Library Association, "To be information literate, a person must be able to recognize when information is needed and have the ability to locate, evaluate, and use effectively the needed information" (1989, par. 3). Researchers have shown that information literacy facilitates personal interests, learning, self-direction, and cultural participation (American Library Association, 2000; Koltay, 2011). The specific ability to search competently is discussed as a component skill of information literacy (e.g., Bawden and Robinson, 2002; Koltay, 2011). In particular, searching for information on the Internet has been associated with facilitating and motivating learning (Kolikant, 2010), and children have reported enjoying researching online (Jewitt and Parashart, 2011). Search literacy, defined here as the ability to understand and use search engines to access information on the Internet, should be considered separately from other digital and media literacy concepts.

As a result of new search technologies and the ever-expanding information landscape that is increasingly accessible for children, adults have the opportunity and responsibility to support children as searchers and consumers of information. Our approach toward search literacy should be to design search interfaces and provide search education for children using methods that meet children at their paths to engagement, preference, and skill. What is needed to accomplish this goal is twofold: first, an understanding of children's stable search patterns, those behaviors that have persisted over time despite changes in technology, and second, an acceptance of search as a whole experience including not only user-interface interactions, but also affective, environmental, cultural, and user belief factors, termed a *child-centric* view. This book focuses on reconciling what is known about children's search from past research with a new, child-centric framework of searcher types.

A CHILD-CENTRIC FRAMING OF RESEARCH

There is a range of search skills that children may have or develop when freely searching the Internet. These can include familiarity with the search interface, foreknowledge of websites as information sources, recognition of advertisements, and the ability to formulate queries (Bilal, 2000; Duarte Torres and Weber, 2011; Kammerer and Bohnacker, 2012; Shenton and Dixon, 2003). However, the experience of search can be impacted not only by specific search skills and deficits, but also emotional reactions during search (Bilal, 2005; Kuhlthau, 1991, 1993; Nahl, 2004), the interests of the searcher, social influences, the searcher's beliefs, and the context and environment of the search (Davies, 2011; Hirsh, 1996; Kuiper et al., 2005; Selwyn et al., 2009). Bilal terms this view of the searcher as a whole, and not simply made up of search skills, behaviors, or emotional reactions as separate parts the "affective paradigm" (Bilal, 2005).

In order to better support children's search literacy through new curriculum, informal learning experiences, and the development of new technologies, it is necessary to conceptualize children's search as a complete experience that is *child-centric* in nature. A child-centric view of young searchers rejects a granular parsing of search behavior into steps or skills in the process of finding information that children can either enact or fail to accomplish. For example, children must transmit a query to a search system in order to enable the system to return results. Whether typing, clicking a subject heading, or verbally querying, judging a child according to notions of skill level or the black and white of success vs. failure is difficult to resist. Todd (2003) described this focus on only user-interface interactions as "atomistic," and contrasted it with a "holistic" focus on the user. A child-centric view of search encompasses the experiences, skills, context, and emotions occurring during search from the point of view of the searcher. While young children may fumble as they search on interfaces aimed at adult users, a child-centric approach for researchers attempting to encourage search literacy seeks out not only areas of deficit but also areas of strength.

To illustrate a child-centric framework to search, consider the following. A 7-year-old searcher predictably might have difficulty reading the results presented on the search results page, making the selection of search results a challenge. In a narrow view, an adult stakeholder might recognize this information acquisition challenge and attempt to implement a solution that addresses reading levels. In contrast, by taking a child-centric view, a researcher may also take into account that the same child searcher can successfully acquire the desired information despite not being able to understand all of the words on the search result page. The searcher might implement strategies to overcome problems on their own: using pre-established search rules for guidance, adding "for kids" to the end of their search query, seeking help from a nearby sibling, or making use of familiar sites. These successful strategies become apparent when broadening the focus from problem identification and instead attempting to observe search as comprised of many problems, solutions, reactions, and interactions.

Within the field of Human-computer Interaction (HCI), the need for a child-centric view of search should be familiar. In a call to apply a broader perspective to research and design, Nardi (1996) described the approaches of activity theory. Activity theory seeks to unite the intentions, background, interactions with others, and change over time in a user with the actions taken by that user. Nardi described, "We have recognized that technology use is not a mechanical input-output relation between a person and a machine; a much richer depiction of the user's situation is needed for design and evaluation." (Nardi, 1996, p. 4). Additionally, the literature surrounding the concept of Universal Design reflects the sentiment of needing a more complete understanding of users as a way to enable design. Universal Design holds that interfaces should be approachable for all people, including children, novice adults, those with disabilities, and older adults (Burgstahler, 2011).

THE CHANGING SEARCH LANDSCAPE

Understanding the larger context surrounding a search experience is critical at a time when children are searching an ever-changing and evolving Internet landscape. In addition, the search tools themselves are evolving as the technology becomes more sophisticated and powerful. Therefore, the search experience reflects a collection of technologically and culturally driven factors that both directly and indirectly affect how users seek information.

For example, it is common practice for search engine developers to frequently and unexpectedly add new or remove tools, change the user experience of existing tools, and move tools to different areas of screen real-estate. Many times, there will be little warning to users, and these subtle changes can either surprisingly enhance or negatively impact a search experience. The changing search landscape can also be seen in the growing importance of social media and social influence. Young people are just not searching on their own. They are reaching out more often to peers, mentors, and through social media in combination with search engines. In addition, children's search experiences are commonly carried out on mobile devices. While device ownership for children is increasing (Lenhart et al., 2010), devices are also frequently shared with family members or used as communal classroom tools. Children who share mobile device access will have more limited opportunities to develop proficiency, and the personalization offered by many devices based on search history or location will not always apply to a particular child. The ever-changing technology landscape demands continual evaluation for changes that affect children's search. In response, we can revise how we conceptualize the process of search and update approaches for educating and designing interfaces to support young searchers.

INTERFACES IN FLUX

A major factor when considering the changing search landscape is how redesigning and updating search interfaces alters the search behaviors of children. The American Library Association (2000) considers information literacy competency present only if a student can search on multiple interfaces and search engines. As the need to develop this skill is explicitly stated, it can be inferred that searching on different interfaces can require significantly different sets of skills. Even slight visual interface changes have the potential to disrupt practiced search habits of young searchers; a shorter or longer search box can alter the length of a query entered by a user and the inclusion of images in results can increase the rates of result clicking (Wilson, 2012, p. 30; 50). Gossen et al. (2012) reported that their flexible, user-customizable visual interface was preferred by children, indicating that children were aware of visual interface elements and appreciated the ability to alter them to suit personal needs. Not all changes in search engines over time are restricted to visual design. Marchionini (2006) discussed advances in search system structures that had the overall goal of drawing users into search as more active and engaged participants, such as supporting multi-phase, social, or iterative learning search tasks. Wilson (2012) noted that changes to the search landscape span not only interface redesigns, but also the growing and waning dominance of various search engine providers, such as Bing, Yahoo!, and Google. This book is notably focused toward the current overwhelmingly dominant commercial search engine, Google, although other interfaces are discussed from prior literature when they relate. (See Figures I.2, I.3, and I.4 for examples of visual interface changes over time in the Google homepage.) As users migrate to and from different search engines over time, it can be expected that children's search behaviors will change as well.

Figure I-2: Google homepage, October 30, 2008, just after beginning data collection for Druin et al. (2010).

Figure I-3: The Google homepage as of June 28, 2013, during data collection for Foss (2014).

Figure I-4: The Google homepage from 2014, current as of July 2014.

SOCIAL MEDIA AND SOCIAL INFLUENCE

Children continually expand and change their social circles, widening their sphere of influence from including only immediate family members at younger ages to encompassing friends, classmates, teachers, and others by mid-adolescence. This is reflected in their increasing reliance on others for assistance in searching and using the Internet for social media. Using social media sites is an increasingly common activity for children (Blackwell et al., 2014; Madden et al., 2012). Although most social media platforms are age-restricted, prohibiting users younger than 13 from joining, children are heavy and frequent users of sites such as Instagram, Facebook, or Google+ (Blackwell et al., 2014; Livingstone et al., 2010). Although social media is separated conceptually from Internet searching, children who develop keen skills navigating social media sites have a number of advantages over children who are not regular users. There is inevitably inappropriate or offensive content on such sites, and children who are exposed to such content can become adept at avoiding it (Valcke et al., 2011). Young social media users also potentially have access to large numbers of online contacts and known and trusted social sites to reach out to when struggling to solve a problem via independent Internet search (Agosto et al., 2012). Social creation leads to new sources for information and new ways for searchers to have to identify what is reliable (Mackey and Jacobson, 2011).

MOBILE

Children are increasingly likely to own or have ready access to a mobile device, and the age at which children begin interacting with these devices is decreasing (Lenhart et al., 2010). Children no longer have to postpone their investigation of a topic of interest until they can reach a desktop computer or find Wi-Fi for a laptop. Instead, they are able to instantly settle arguments, help each other with school assignments, and connect to a larger world by searching using smartphones or tablets from their schools, friends' homes, shopping malls, or bedrooms (Lampe et al., 2012).

Much research in the area of younger children and mobile devices focuses on engagement with games and educational apps, while for older children, social media is often discussed (e.g., Common Sense Media, 2013). Existing research on mobile search user interfaces acknowledges that changes are likely as technology advances, and that there is the opportunity for designers to facilitate search literacy in innovative ways (Wilson, 2012).

PREVIEW OF BOOK

In Chapter 1, we present the various approaches to studying children's search from past research with a summary chart included for reference. We then characterize the current search experience for children when using mainstream commercial search engines such as Google. Following this in Chapter 2, the research approach we have taken at the University of Maryland is described, as is the search role framework we have developed to classify child searchers. The search role framework describes eight archetypes, or "search roles," for child searchers. The most prominent characteristics of each search role are described based on the work of Druin et al. (2010), Foss et al. (2012, 2013), and Foss (2014).

The search role framework is used as a lens for examining children's search for the chapters that follow. In specific, Chapters 3–5 focus on using the framework to parse the previous literature, finding further evidence for each role from past studies as well as providing a strong perspective with which to conduct future research. The book concludes with a summary of the discussion from each chapter, a broader discussion of the roles and their affinity to each other, the applicability of the framework for different stakeholders, and implications for the future of children's Internet search research.

CHAPTER 1

Existing Research

1.1 APPROACHES OF THE EXISTING RESEARCH

Within the body of existing literature, different researchers have taken varied approaches to exploring how children engage as searchers. First, studies have examined children's information seeking using different technology systems. Over time, the research has evolved with the currently available search systems, moving from children's use of Online Public Access Catalogues (OPACs) to search portals designed to return preselected and curated documents for children, and more recently, to children's searching on the open and unrestricted Internet using adult-oriented search interfaces. Second, the scope of existing research has not always been consistent. Existing studies range from intensive analyses of fragments of the search process to exhaustive descriptions of whole search processes in children. Third, the research setting has often varied. Researchers have engaged children with search technologies in public schools, laboratories, and public libraries. Finally, most studies have been limited in their participant enrollment, both in the number and in the age of participants. Enrolling small numbers of participants has allowed researchers to understand nuanced behaviors, but narrowed their ability to establish patterns across large numbers of children. However, the existing literature falls short of arriving at a complete description of children's engagement with Internet search in the current search landscape.

1.1.1 SEARCH SYSTEM TECHNOLOGY

In the past, research on children's engagement with search interfaces has been dependent on the technology available at the time. Search technologies have advanced over time, such as during the brief popularity of CD-ROM encyclopedias and children's search portals occurring between OPACs and the Internet. While many findings arising from studies of children searching on now-outdated systems are still relevant, many are not. For example, many studies discuss the use (or lack of use) of Boolean logic (e.g., Borgman et al., 1995; Large et al., 1998; Kafai and Bates, 1997; Schacter et al., 1998; Shenton and Dixon, 2003), although these operators are no longer necessary for success using current search engines. Additionally, the search systems used in these studies often relied on closed datasets of possible results (e.g., Abbas, 2005; Bilal, 2000, 2001, 2002; Borgman et al., 1995; Large et al., 1998; Marchionini, 1989). Such preselected sets of documents ensured that children were able to retrieve results appropriate in both content and reading level, but do not provide a good analogy to search on the open Internet. A study using only preselected content conducted in the current open-Internet search landscape would be similar to researchers in decades past permitting children to only retrieve books from three shelves in a library.

1.1.2   RESEARCH SCOPE

Past research has had various focal points of study. Some researchers have intensely studied a piece of the search process. For example, Kammerer and Bohnacker (2012) and Abbas (2005) looked only at children's query formulation and other researchers have focused on result selection (Dinet et al., 2010; Hirsh, 1999). These studies provide valuable insight for the areas of their focus, but are difficult to assimilate into a larger picture of children's search. In contrast, much research has had a broad scope and characterized search behaviors in general or attempted to synthesize all the search behaviors children display into a process. Fidel et al. (1999) observed the searching of high school students in order to understand their search strategies. Taken together, Bilal's three studies of children searching on Yahooligans! (2000, 2001, 2002) provide an exhaustive description of search skills, emotions, and physical behaviors in seventh grade students. Solomon (1993) conducted a large-scale study of participants of a range of ages conducting searches, and presented results spanning many aspects of search, including navigation, query formulation, and search breakdowns. Studies with a broad scope are often so encompassing that it makes it difficult to derive typical or simplified patterns of search behavior for children.

Additionally, longitudinal research with the goal of understanding how children change as searchers over time is an extremely important area to explore. However, in the existing searching literature with children ages 7–17, there is a distinct lack of longitudinal work to establish how search behaviors change in individual or panels of children over time. While some researchers have engaged participants in repeated interventions, their focus was either not on Internet search (Davies, 2011), not on identifying change in search behavior over time (Bilal, 2000, 2001, 2002), or with adult participants (Anick and Kantamneni, 2008; Nahl, 2004). Longitudinal research to understand children and adolescent's Internet search processes has the potential to make a much larger impact than research conducted at a single point in time. Longitudinal research allows for understanding patterns of change through time, whether specific effects increase or decrease, and if change does occur, the magnitude of the change (Menard, 2002). Establishing what search behaviors, values, and habits are consistent or prone to change in children when considering age and factors in the larger technology landscape provides insights when attempting to promote better search interface design and search literacy. For example, longitudinal research demonstrating that a particular negative search habit is present only for very young searchers can help adult stakeholders to avoid wasting resources to extinguish a habit that will perish on its own. Conversely, search habits, positive or negative, that are revealed as persisting across all ages and over time are obvious areas for education and engaging children with Internet search.

1.1.3   RESEARCH SETTINGS

Research on children's Internet search should take place in the physical spaces children and adolescents most often choose to engage with search. In the past, most research took place in the context of the school or public library, with research in the homes of children being almost non-existent. At the time in which early search studies were conducted, school-based research made sense, as children were most likely to engage with search systems in their schools to complete school assignments. However, educational settings can impose restrictions on children when searching (Gross, 2006; Selwyn et al., 2009) and possibly elicit search strategies not employed by choice (Fidel et al., 1999). Purcell et al. (2012) reported that teachers are beginning to allow students to use personal cell phones and other mobile devices to access the Internet during class time, but there is little research as yet on this type of search. Recently, home Internet penetration has expanded (Davies, 2011; Rideout et al., 2010), and children and adolescents more frequently engage with general search at home (Selwyn et al., 2009). Thus, schools no longer provide the most logical setting for exploring children's search.

Search in the home environment differs notably from search in the school environment in terms of the time, content restrictions, and topics children and adolescents are given when searching. First, in the home setting, children are able to engage with Internet search under fewer time limitations than in school (Agosto, 2002: Rideout et al., 2010). This gives young searchers the freedom to pursue tangential or personally interesting topics, as they do not have to rush to complete an assignment. Second, parental rules regarding permissible online interactions for children of all ages largely depend on monitoring, co-use of the computer, or on parental trust in adolescents (Livingstone and Helsper, 2008; Shenton and Dixon, 2003). In contrast, schools rely heavily on unilateral content filtering software to regulate online activities of students (Selwyn et al., 2009). As a result, children searching in the home have far more flexibility in the content they can access. Finally, in the school setting, children and adolescents frequently search on imposed or assigned tasks (Gross, 2006). Children can perceive this type of search with disengagement or a lack of motivation (Davies, 2011), which is tied to search success (van der Sluis and van Dijk, 2010). Children and adolescents can also respond to imposed topics by being highly focused and unwilling to deviate from teacher guidelines, as these guidelines determine the ultimate grade awarded by the teacher (Chung and Neuman, 2007; Fidel et al., 1999). When searching at home, children are more able use the Internet in the way they choose to search for topics driven by personal interest (Davies, 2011; Selwyn et al., 2009; Shenton and Dixon, 2003).

1.1.4   NUMBER AND AGE OF PARTICIPANTS

There are several reasons to limit the number of participants in a qualitative research study. A single individual's interview with researchers requires hours devoted later to analysis. Data saturation, the point at which no new information relevant to the research questions is uncovered within a dataset, can be reached early if research goals and data collection methods are tightly focused. Certain age or other demographic factors may act as boundaries for participation, and recruitment may therefore be difficult or intentionally limited. In Participatory Design, a potential approach to improving search interfaces for children, members of a user group interact on equal footing with researchers to create technology and interfaces that better meet their needs. For Participatory Design research, small numbers of users act as representatives for their user group, and involving many participants is unwieldy.

Given these considerations, it is not surprising that most researchers studying children's Internet search have involved relatively few participants in their work. The median number of participants included in prior research on children's search has been just over 30, with few studies enrolling larger numbers of children and adolescents. Often, the low number of participants has been tied to the research setting of the school, as a school's computer lab housed a certain number of computers or because a participating classroom had a specific number of students. Other studies on children's search have intentionally enrolled small participant groups for Participatory Design studies (Large et al., 2004) or to act as usability testers for a newly designed search interface. Other studies have included child searchers incidentally as they visited a public library, targeting all age groups and ensnaring a few children by chance (Slone, 2003).

With some exceptions, most research examined participants of particular and proximal age ranges, focusing on either children or adolescents, but not both (see Table 1.1). This has resulted in a lack of understanding of changes in search behavior over time arising due more to aging than to research method, research goal, employed search system, or setting.

1.1.5   SUMMARY OF EXISTING APPROACHES

The following table (Table 1.1) summarizes prior research studies conducted specifically with child participants and with research goals surrounding understanding aspects of search. Many studies include discussions of children's engagement with the Internet in general and touch on children's searching. However, these studies are excluded from the summary below as their main area of focus is not on search. Also excluded are meta-reviews of the search literature, commentaries on children's search, or studies using query logs as sources for data rather than child participants, although these are valuable resources as well.

Table 1.1: Prior research studies focusing on children and search

Authors	Year	Search System	Research Goal	Setting	Enrolled	Ages
Abbas	2005	Preselected content	Compare children's stated search questions with their entered queries	School	754	11–13
Agosto	2002	Preselected sites	Explore adolescent girls' Web-based decision making	Lab	22	14–16
Bar-Ilan and Belous	2007	Preselected content	Determine children's preferred subject organization	Home	48	9–11
Bilal	2000	Preselected content	Understand search behaviors, including navigation for fact-based search tasks	School	22	12–13
Bilal	2001	Preselected content	Understand search behaviors, including navigation for research tasks	School	17	12–13
Bilal	2002	Preselected content	Understand search behaviors, including navigation for self-generated search tasks	School	22	12–13
Bilal and Wang	2005	Preselected content	Understand how children categorize related concepts to inform search directory hierarchy design	School	11	12–13
Borgman et al.	1995	Preselected content	Search and browse metrics to optimize search system design for children	School; public library	34	9–12
Bowler	2010	Open: Internet, books, etc.	Examine cognitive behaviors and affect during search	School; phone interview; diary	10	16–18
Chung and Neuman	2007	Open: Databases, Internet, books, etc.	Adolescent search processes on self-generated tasks	School	21	16–17

Cooper	2002	Internet, books	Compare search behaviors for books and electronic sources	School	21	7
Dinet et al.	2010	Internet	Children's visual examination of results pages	School	89	10–17
Eickhoff et al.	2012	Internet	Automatically classify children into search roles using detailed search metrics	School	29	9–13
Fidel et al.	1999	Internet	Establish general adolescent Web search behaviors	School	8	16–18
Gossen et al.	2012	Preselected content	Compare new interface designed for children with existing search engines	Lab	28	7–12
Hirsh	1996	Preselected content	Understand children's search in electronic environments	School	54	10–11
Hirsh	1999	Open: Internet, online catalogue, electronic encyclope-dia	Understand children's relevance criteria and search processes	School	10	10–11
Hutchinson et al.	2007	Preselected content	Compare hierarchical or flat category structures	School	72	6–11
Jochmann-Mannak et al.	2010	Internet	Compare Internet with children's search interfaces	School	32	8–12
Jochmann-Mannak et al.	2014	Preselected websites	Comparison of children's affective responses to playful website design	School	158	10–12
Kafai and Bates	1997	Internet	How children view the organization of information on the Internet	School	166	6–12
Kammerer and Bohnacker	2012	Internet	Compare NL and keyword querying	Lab	21	8–10

Large, Beheshti and Breuleux	1998	Preselected content	How children search using electronic resources	School	53	11–12
Large and Beheshti	2000	Open: Web, print, CD-ROM	Comparison of web and print materials for school assignments	School	53	11–12
Large, Beheshti and Rahman	2002	Preselected content	Compare children's search interfaces and elicit design suggestions	School	23	10–13
Marchionini	1989	Preselected content	Success measures; search patterns; query formulation	School	52	8–12
Nesset	2013	Open: Web, print	Holistically model information seeking of students in the school setting	School	52	8–9
Schacter et al.	1998	Internet	Comparison of process on ill- or well-defined tasks	School; personal computer	32	10–12
Shenton and Dixon	2003	Internet and CD-ROM	Comparison of Internet and CD-ROM	School	188	3–18
Slone	2002	Web and online catalogue	How age, goals, and experience affect Web/online catalog search	Public library	11	7–17
Solomon	1993	Preselected content	Overall successes and breakdowns; navigation	School	679	6–12

1.2 CHILDREN'S CURRENT EXPERIENCE OF SEARCH

Children perceive and use search interfaces differently than adults, and an awareness of their perceptions of the current search landscape can prove to be revealing. For example, when presented with a results page, often Wikipedia is the first result listed. Adults find this to be useful and often locate needed information within Wikipedia. For younger children, however, not only is the vocabulary of Wikipedia often at a level too difficult to easily comprehend, but there is also the ever-present search rule of "Don't use Wikipedia" (Foss, 2014). Even the icons used in search interfaces can be confusing for children. For adults, Google's current microphone icon evokes nostalgic images of early radio. But from the point of view of a child, the icon more closely resembles a tulip than the microphone toy with which a child would be familiar from childhood play (Figure 1.1). Almost all children share some common struggles with current search systems, such as with interpreting and selecting results, with using input devices, and with spelling. They also have commonalities in online content creation, responses to minor interventions, and in visual design preferences.

Figure 1.1: Comparison of a tulip, Google's microphone icon, and a toy microphone. Images: freefoto.com, iconfinder.com, http://www.theshoppingmama.com.

1.2.1   CHILDREN AND RESULTS INTERPRETATION

On the Google search results page, each result has four major components of importance to the participants in the searching studies. The first component of a result is the page title, displayed in underlined blue text, indicating that the title is a clickable link. Second (at least for 2013; this was placed lower in 2008) is the URL of the page, displayed in green text. In black text are snippets, or excerpts, from the website text containing the query terms. Finally, the query terms are displayed in bold text when they appear in the page title or in the snippet. Figure 1.2 displays a search result containing these four elements: page title, URL, snippet, and bolded search terms. It should be noted that some specific types of results, such as those for blogs or news items, have additional components.

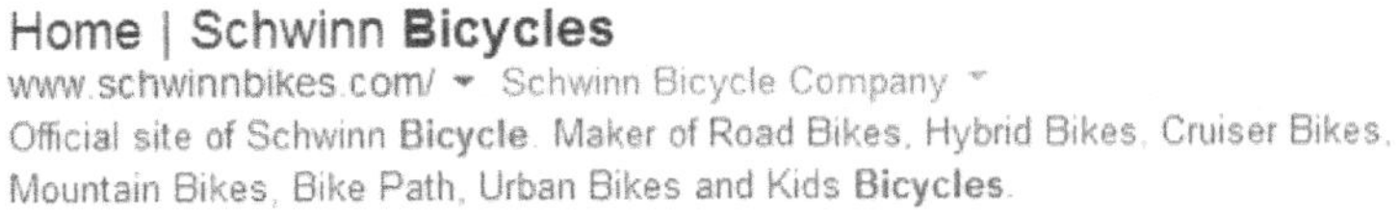

Home | Schwinn **Bicycles**
www.schwinnbikes.com/ ▾ Schwinn Bicycle Company ▾
Official site of Schwinn **Bicycle**. Maker of Road Bikes, Hybrid Bikes, Cruiser Bikes,
Mountain Bikes, Bike Path, Urban Bikes and Kids **Bicycles**.

Figure 1.2: Google search result. Example search result containing the page title in blue text, the page URL in green text, the snippet from the website containing the query terms, and the query terms in bolded text. Retrieved June 2014.

Studying children's engagement with search results pages reveals definite layout preferences. Bilal (2012) summarizes her own series of studies on children's searching for different types of tasks, describing that children were most likely to select results near the top of the results page rather than farther down the results page. Other researchers have further confirmed via children's query logs that young searchers do not explore past the first page of results (Duarte Torres et al., 2010). Druin et al. (2009) confirmed children's rank-based selection preferences and low likelihood of viewing multiple pages of results.

Children and adolescents are not universally adept at understanding search engine results pages. When it comes to individual search results, children have difficulty judging whether retrieved documents are relevant to their information needs (Jochmann-Mannak et al., 2010; van der Sluis and van Dijk, 2010). Children look to find their keywords and explicit answers to their queries in the text on the results page (Hirsh, 1999; van der Sluis and van Dijk, 2010), and often, answers can only be obtained by clicking through to websites.

Children's reliance on results page text is documented in other research as well; Collins-Thompson et al. (2011) explored the behavior of searchers within a search log dataset when the website title and snippet on the results page were of a lower reading level than the content on the associated website. They found that when the reading level of the results page text did not match the associated website, searchers spent much less time engaging with the website. For young children, then, it is highly important that the results page information contain entered keywords and closely mirror the content of the associated websites. Additionally, children under the age of 11 in Foss (2014) were not highly aware of URLs, and did not report using the URL as selection criteria when choosing a result. Rather than presenting URLs as a major component of the search result, search engine results could use text to describe the source of the information, which is occasionally not included in the page title. As older children do find URLs to be useful (Foss, 2014), rather than excluding them, they could be moved to less prominent positioning within the search result, as in Figure 1.3.

Giant **Panda** Facts - National Zoo - Smithsonian Institution

nationalzoo.si.edu/.../GiantPandas/... ▾ Smithsonian National Zoological Park ▾

The giant **panda**, a black-and-white **bear**, has a body typical of **bears**. It has black fur on
ears, eye patches, muzzle, legs, and shoulders. The rest of the animal's ...

Giant **Panda** Facts - National Zoo - Smithsonian Institution

Smithsonian National Zoological Park ▾   nationalzoo.si.edu/.../Giant**Pandas**/... ▾

The giant **panda**, a black-and-white **bear**, has a body typical of **bears**. It has black fur on
ears, eye patches, muzzle, legs, and shoulders. The rest of the animal's ...

Figure 1.3: Possibility for a minor change to Google's search results that children would find helpful:
switching the source with the URL.

1.2.2   TYPING, MOUSING, AND SPELLING CHALLENGES

Entering text into a search system via typing on a keyboard has been found repeatedly to be a
difficult task for children, particularly under the age of 10. Children have been reported to have
trouble locating keys, a preference for touchscreens, a preference for the autocomplete function,
and frustration with typing (Borgman et al., 1995; Foss, 2014; Jochmann-Mannak et al., 2010;
Large et al., 2004; Solomon, 1993). Children also have difficulty with input via a mouse. Children,
in comparison to adults, are significantly slower to click targets, and have less ability to move the
mouse in a direct line (Borgman et al., 1995; Hourcade et al., 2004).

Spelling difficulties are likewise a prevalent finding, and one that seems to persist despite
vast improvements in search interfaces being able to compensate for poorly spelled queries. Solomon (1993) and Fidel et al. (1999) both found in research with students of broad ages that spelling errors persisted even for older children. Gossen et al. (2011) stated that queries generated by
children within a query log dataset contained spelling errors 40% of the time as compared to the
10–15% of erroneous adult-entered queries quoted by other researchers. In another recent study,
Barsky and Bar-Ilan (2012) also reported their participants having difficulty with spelling, as did
Druin et al. (2009).

1.2.3   CREATION

Children use computers and devices to create new artifacts (Foss, 2014; Shenton, 2008). This finding is important to note in that children are creating not only artifacts to print and use outside of
the computer environment, but they are comfortable with creating artifacts that exist only within
the bounds of the computer. These artifacts—playlists, collections of images, websites—represent
a way to motivate children toward computer use. Leveraging the intersection between technology

and ownership of new content can spark interest in search and extend expertise gained from tools used for creation into search skills.

1.2.4   IMPACT OF MINOR INTERVENTIONS

A small number of participants during Foss (2014) were new to Internet search, and as part of the interview script, when these novice searchers were unable to navigate to a search engine, the researchers briefly introduced Google. They demonstrated how to navigate to the Google homepage, how to type a query, and explained the websites and images on the results page were clickable for more information. Some of the participants who were introduced to Google during their 2008 interviews remembered learning to search from the researchers as 2013 participants, recalling the brief tutorial occurring years prior and citing it as how they learned to search. In the context of search education, this is an encouraging finding, as it demonstrates that even minor early interventions by adults can have long-lasting effects on children. Conversely, children may recall detrimental interventions in the same way as they remembered helpful ones.

Given the enthusiasm of almost all children for technology, the Internet, and search, it is clear that children are unlikely to be deterred from using computers, tablets, and smartphones. Even when faced with changes in interfaces and devices, children persist in their desire to use technology. When considering how to support children to become more search literate, it is encouraging to know that a single bad experience is unlikely to create a reluctant or disengaged searcher.

1.2.5   VISUAL DESIGN PREFERENCES

Redesigning small visual aspects of search interfaces using the lens of children's experiences would lead to significant improvements in usability for young searchers. In addition to children's differing perceptions, children prefer to search according to criteria not represented within traditional interfaces (Druin, 2005). Hutchinson et al. (2007) discussed that young children select books from physical shelves based on the book cover features such as illustrations or predominant color. Transplanting these findings to the Internet and the search engine results page, children do not have a parallel to colorful covers and drawings within the search interface, possibly making it difficult to choose one visually monotonous result over another.

However, children do change their search behavior based on interface changes, as shown repeatedly throughout the research literature. For example, children in Foss (2014) discussed YouTube much more often after a link to the site was added directly to the Google homepage. Children in Bilal (2000) who lacked existing interface knowledge were less successful searchers. Dinet et al. (2010) discussed children altering their interpretation of the search engine results page based on visual cues such as bolded text. Certainty in visual interface design decisions is needed prior to making changes, as changes undoubtedly affect young searchers.

1.3   CLASSIFYING ADULT SEARCHERS

The existing research for adults as searchers has advanced further than the researcher for children. For adults, there seems to be a trend toward creating classification systems of types of searchers. These systems rely on established knowledge regarding how adults approach searching. There is little need for reevaluation of the basic assumptions of adult search, as repeated research on the topic over time has resolved any lingering debates. For children, repeated studies have likewise shown similar results. However, a coherent system to conceptualize children as searchers has not arisen in the previous literature.

Singer et al. (2012), pointed out that broader use of the Internet in recent years by different groups raises the need to attempt a classification of those users. "In doing so, it becomes possible to understand different uses, maximize the possible support efforts and target content to particular needs. (Literature review section, para. 1)." In adults, there have been previous studies that have organized people into searcher categories based on patterns of searching behavior. Singer et al. (2012) used six user profiles to examine performance on simple or complex search tasks. The six types defined are:

- **Active versatile Internet users,** who are active in both information seeking, communication and entertainment related use;

- **Practical work oriented Internet users,** who are mainly active information-oriented users;

- **Entertainment oriented active Internet users,** whose main interests include entertainment and communication related uses, and seeking Internet solutions that cater to their interests;

- **Practical information oriented small-scale Internet users** differ from the previous group in that while their activities focus mainly on information use, they are less frequent in their activities;

- **Entertainment and communication oriented small-scale Internet users** also use the Internet less frequently than their active counterparts. Their use focuses on leisure-related activities and they are passive when it comes to information-related activities; and

- **Small-scale Internet users** use the technologies so infrequently that they do not have any significant types of activities that would describe them, and have very poorly developed online behavior. (Singer et al., 2012, Literature review section, para. 3).

In research by Bateman et al. (2012), the authors used three archetypes of adult searchers drawn from prior literature. This approach enabled users to compare their search behaviors with the archetypes to allow for search reflection and improvement. The archetypes accounted for different types of search behaviors that were observable in query logs, notably behaviors that were *techniques* employed by the searcher (e.g., using search operators like "+"), *tendencies* of the searcher (e.g., average length of queries used), and *topics* or domains preferred by the searcher. Using these varied search behaviors to establish common patterns, the authors were able to categorize searchers into three groups: Typical Users, Search Experts, and Topic Experts (Bateman et al., 2012). Another study, sponsored by the BBC, invited members of the public to conduct web searches during a live and filmed experiment (Nicholas et al., 2011). Researchers determined that the participants were most diverse as searchers based on three factors: time spent searching, the ability to multitask, and the importance of social networks. Using these characteristics as the basis for their framework, the researchers identified eight "species of web animal[s]," which are quoted below (Nicholas et al., 2011, p. 31):

- **Web hedgehog.** Hedgehogs are careful Internet users, taking their time to find the right information. They prefer to go it alone, rarely relying on social networks and are specialised web users, best suited to concentrating on one thing at a time. The pilot study found that web hedgehogs tend to be the less-experienced web users.

- **Web fox.** Web foxes are good at finding information quickly. They are highly social, maintaining complex relationships with the other members of their social group, often using social networks, or other sites whose content is created by its users, as sources of information. Web foxes are multi-taskers, able to do several things at the same time. The pilot study found that web foxes tend to be younger (16–24), less experienced web users.

- **Web bear.** Web bears like to browse the Internet at a leisurely pace. They tend to be solitary animals and when they are looking for information, they are less likely to use social networks. Web bears are highly adaptable multi-taskers, able to do several things at the same time. The pilot study found that web bears tend to be older (30+) and female.

- **Web leopard.** Web leopards are adept at getting information from the Internet very quickly. The web leopard likes to go it alone when looking for information, and they are best suited to performing one task at a time. In the pilot study we found that web leopards tend to be young (16–24) and male.

- **Web elk.** Web elks take their time finding exactly the right information. They are social creatures but perform best when they focus on one thing at a time, rather than trying to multitask. The pilot study found that web elks tend to be more experienced, older users.

- **Web octopus**. Web octopuses surf fast and when looking for information they tend to go it alone rather than rely on social networks. Web octopuses are highly adaptable and show a range of sophisticated online behaviors, successfully keeping track of several different things simultaneously. In the pilot study, web octopuses tended to be young (16–24), male and spend a lot of time online.

- **Web ostrich.** Web ostriches are speedy surfers and take full advantage of social networks when looking for information. The web ostrich is a true specialist. They are focused and do best when they concentrate on one task at a time. In the pilot study, ostrich-type users tended to be young (16–24), male and spend a lot of time online.

- **Web elephant.** Web elephants browse the Internet at a stately, methodical pace. They often use social networking sites to keep track of friends or family and are happy to rely on information from sites whose content is created by its users. Web elephants are well-suited to carrying out several different tasks at the same time. The pilot study suggested that web elephants are often older, more experienced web users.

These few examples show the efforts undertaken by researchers to further understand Internet searching behavior in adults. The search role framework presented in this book applies the same concepts to the search behavior of children.

1.4   CLASSIFYING CHILD SEARCHERS

Many researchers using varied technologies, research scope, settings, and participant enrollment have found the same patterns or trends in children's Internet search reflected over time (e.g., Rowlands et al., 2008). If taken in its entirety, the prior body of literature builds a foundational understanding of children's search interactions. So what is missing? There has been little aggregation of the fragmented observations of dozens of researchers into a single, cohesive theory of children's Internet search as it presents in the current search landscape. Especially interesting is that some of the same patterns are found regardless of decade; children searching on an OPAC share some behaviors with those using the open Internet. How is it possible that children from different geographic locations and settings of search, with differing familiarity and comfort searching, of different ages, and of different *generations* all produce the same researcher observations? And if these unfocused and echoed researcher observations were to be collated away from the noise of the divergent scopes of their studies, would a cross-study and previously unseen pattern emerge?

To pursue commonalities, we read across what we believe to be the entire body of existing studies on child and adolescent search behaviors. This review of the literature did seem to reveal a subtle and unnoticed pattern. Many studies directly examine children's Internet search behavior, while others examine children's Internet habits, media use, or educational benefits gained from online resources. The literature contains repeated descriptions of unique groups of children: participants who are similar to each other and different from other groups based on their behaviors, skills, verbalizations, beliefs, or emotions while searching. These disparate groupings of children are often mentioned in passing or anecdotally, usually as contrasts between one or two sets of participants. For example:

- "…it appears that these young people's attitudes and uses of new technologies tended to develop in one of two distinct directions…" (Davies, 2011, p. 334);

- "…it is possible to divide the students into three groups…" (Large and Beheshti, 2000, p. 1072);

- "In short, there are patterns of similarity and variety across the grade levels and among the sexes that reflect both common and diverse interests as well as the curriculum." (Solomon, 1993, p. 261);

- "…we see that young people can be categorised into four distinct profiles based on the ways that they use the Internet and that there are specific individual and contextual factors that help us to understand the likely characteristics of the individuals." (Eynon and Malberg, 2011, p. 593); and

- "Three patterns have been discerned: fast surfing, broad scanning, and deep diving. The search goal is characteristic for the pattern, respectively: finishing the search as quickly as possible, finding as much information as possible, trying to understand." (van der Sluis and van Dijk, 2010)

Through our longitudinal research studies at the University of Maryland, we believe we have been able to uncover patterns in children's search and that these patterns are reflected in the prior literature. These patterns allow us to group children as searchers into search roles. Chapter 2 will detail the methods of our research and present the search role framework resulting from our work.

University of Maryland's Children and Internet Search Studies and the Search Role Framework

Since 2008, at the University of Maryland we have explored how children search the Internet (Druin et al., 2009, 2010; Foss et al., 2012, 2013; Foss, 2014). We conducted the first iteration of our research with 83 children, and returned to 50 of the same participants approximately 4 years later to examine searching changes in the home context. Our focus was not on documenting portions of the search process, but rather on understanding child searchers from a child-centric perspective. Our team of researchers sought to understand emotional reactions and beliefs, interactions with the interface and other people, and progressive steps taken to reach a conclusion to the search from parent and child participants in the home setting. The outcome of this approach was a framework of search roles displayed by children when searching.

2.1 METHODS

2.1.1 RECRUITMENT

At the start of our research in 2008, child and parent participants were recruited via the authors' social networks, by posting flyers, and by electronic mailing lists. These children and parents lived primarily in the suburban Maryland area, with some participants from rural Virginia, one from Washington DC, and one from Delaware. It was necessary for participants to have home Internet access in order to participate.

Recruitment for the second iteration of the research in 2013 was based on the 2008 list of parent participants, with contact done primarily through email. Telephone was used with participants who did not respond by email. Recruitment was hampered by the lack of updated contact information due to the span of time between the studies (three or four years, depending on whether the original interview occurred at the beginning or end of the initial year-long study). To address this challenge, we used our personal networks to reach some participants. Researchers did not offer incentives for participation during either study.

2.1.2 PARTICIPANTS

Participating children in 2008 were ages 7, 9, or 11 to allow for meaningful differences across ages to surface. Children separated in age by only a few months would likely have similar search behaviors, but by including distinctly separate ages, there was an increased likelihood of observing how children changed as searchers as they aged. Over the course of a year, 83 children were enrolled in the study along with at least one parent per child participant, for a total of 170 individual participants. Most child participants attended public schools, although some were homeschooled.

All of the participants in 2013 were returning participants from our 2008 study, and therefore form a panel for longitudinal examination (Saldaña, 2003). These participants in the intervening years had aged to between 10 and 15 years old but remained in 3 age groupings. See Table 2.1 for the ages of the participants over time. Fifty-one of the original 83 participants were reenrolled, resulting in a child participant retention rate of 61%. One longitudinal interview was discarded because we were unable to complete the interview. The child participant had moved to another state so Skype was used for the interview, however, due to poor connection speed there was no way to complete the data collection.

Table 2.1: Participant age groupings over time		
Age Group	2008 Age	2013 Age
Youngest	7	10–11
Middle	9	12–13
Oldest	11	14–15

2.1.3 DATA COLLECTION

At each home, researchers first conducted parent interviews with the child out of the room to gain background on each child's computer use habits, as well as to provide corroboration for some of the information asked during the child interviews. The parent interview script was the same for all parents and included questions about the child's computer and search experience level, frustrations, house rules, and concluded with the parent's occupation and self-assessment of their own computer skill level. Other demographic information such as ethnicity or income was not collected, as researchers felt that this could be perceived by the participating families as invasive. Researchers audio recorded the parent interviews.

Following the parent interview, researchers interviewed the child while he or she used the home computer with which they had the highest level of comfort or familiarity. Researchers videotaped the child interviews, and were careful to position the video camera during the child interviews from a side perspective, recording both the child and the computer screen to allow for capturing maximum data that included the child's interaction with the computer and the physical space of the interview. The interview protocol, which was the same for all children, consisted of three main sections. Beginning with general searching experience questions, the interview then segued into six searching tasks. The interview tasks included *self-generated* and *imposed tasks*. The imposed tasks were further defined by whether they were *one-step* (simple) or *complex* (multi-step) tasks. Self-generated tasks, as they were proposed by the participants, varied in complexity. During the interview, the search tasks were ordered to allow for an increasingly detailed view of each participant's search preference and skill, since the tasks became more specific as the interview progressed. The interview script concluded with general opinion questions about Google, the overwhelming search engine of preference, search frustration, and a question asking the participant to describe an ideal searching tool.

Each type of search task was included to provide a complete picture of how the participants would search given a variety of contexts. The self-generated questions were included to observe the children searching in the most naturalistic fashion possible despite the interview setting. Imposed tasks allowed ease of comparison across individuals, as each participant was presented with the same task. However, it should be noted that these tasks were somewhat artificial, as children frequently have adult assistance available to them in a way the researchers did not offer, and because actual imposed tasks often are much more nuanced than those used in the study. One-step search tasks allowed researchers to observe typical search habits such as browser and search engine choice, as well as skill and familiarity with search and the computer. The complex search tasks established the upper threshold of search skill and the participant's ability to parse tasks into small pieces.

The tasks from 2013 were not identical to those from 2008, and there were some changes to the other interview questions as well. During the 2013 research, researchers used an updated version of the 2008 study protocol, which included new questions, slightly altered search tasks (to search for a different animal than before, for example) and an entirely new and more difficult search task. The intentions for each search task asked of participants are presented in Table 2.2.

Table 2.2: Intended purpose of search tasks		
Task	**Intended Purpose**	**Type of Task**
How do you usually search on the Internet?	Establish preferences and search knowledge	Self-generated
Can you look for information on dolphins/squirrels?	Spelling challenge; approach to broad topic	Imposed; one-step
Can you look for information on what dolphins/squirrels eat?	Approach to narrower topic; navigation; ability to locate relevant information	Imposed; one-step

If you searched on Google for something for your own interest that you never searched for before, what would it be?	Uncover interests; prevent rote repetition of prior search; opportunity for engagement with search	Self-generated
Which day of the week will the Vice President's birthday be on next year?	Task parsing; natural language vs. keyword query formulation	Imposed; complex
(2013 only) Was Michael Jackson's music more popular in 1983 or 2009? Why?	Task parsing; comparison of information; decision criteria based on found information	Imposed; complex

2.1.4   ANALYSIS

Data resulting from the home interviews included parent interview notes, parent interview audio recordings, child interview notes, and child interview video recordings. The notes generated from the interviews provided information such as clicking behavior, spelling of queries, and exact query entries of the participants, as these details can be difficult to capture via video recording. In conjunction with a local transcription service, researchers transcribed all the child and parent interview recordings. The transcripts provided a faithful representation of the dialogue of each interview.

At the first stage of analysis, the transcripts were coded within NVivo data analysis software (QSR International, 2013). Coding began with organizing the participant answers to interview questions into categories. Using methods outlined by Strauss and Corbin (1998) in an emergent coding procedure, over time, researchers began to observe patterns in individual children (e.g., following a rule to guide all search tasks) and among children (e.g., many children following the same rule). Combining the transcript coding with observation of the video and note data allowed researchers to continue to build on and refine the coding categories, following the iterative procedure of Grounded Theory through open coding, axial coding, and selective coding (Strauss and Corbin, 1998).

To develop profiles of each search role in children spanning ages 7–15, Foss (2014) assessed the most distinct search behaviors displayed by children. When a particular group of children displayed a high magnitude of difference (positive or negative) for a particular behavior from other children and the difference persisted over time, the behavior served as an identifying characteristic for the search roles. For example, one group of children were more aware of features of the search engine Google in comparison to other children when first interviewed, and these children remained highly aware of search engine features during their second interviews. This persistent difference thus served as an identifying characteristic for children in the Power Searcher role. Some roles proved to be easily identified, while others required careful observation of subtle search habits or approaches to specific tasks. Additionally, some roles had many identifiable characteristics while other roles stood apart on only a few, although critical, behaviors.

2.1.5   LIMITATIONS

There are noted risks to longitudinal research, namely that by re-enrolling the same participants, they become non-representative of the general population of children with home access to the Internet (LeCompte and Preissle, 1993). Further, due to the difficulty in observing social behaviors directly during an interview setting, most data regarding the social use of the computer in the interview participants was collected anecdotally from participant testimony. This phenomena should be noted for later in the book when Social Searchers are discussed.

Finally, it should be noted that our work at the University of Maryland has been funded by Google Faculty Research Awards throughout the years. To reduce the conflict caused by the funding source, we were careful when interviewing participants to not verbally refer to Google prior to the participant freely choosing to use Google to search. Two search tasks did direct the participants to use Google to allow for ease of comparison of search behaviors, but these tasks occurred late in the interview, after the participants had the opportunity to establish their preferred method of search.

2.2   THE SEARCH ROLE FRAMEWORK

The importance of the search role framework discussed in this book is multifaceted. Roles function to help adult stakeholders in understanding areas of search deficit or strength in children, allowing for targeted interventions in education, parenting, interface design, or research approach. Roles also frame preferences for information presentation in individual children and adolescents, which can confirm for children their ideal approaches to information search tasks. Commonalities spanning multiple roles point to particularly worthwhile areas for intervention, and traits unique to one role show when a tighter focus is needed to support children. Overall, search roles facilitate achieving the central goals of improving search literacy, more accessibility to information, and designing ideal search interfaces for children. Search roles can differentiate children and allow targeted approaches to improving search skills and increasing information access.

The following table, Table 2.3, presents each of the groupings of roles, the eight roles, and the most prominent search behaviors for each role. As defined in our research, search behaviors are observable verbalizations, actions, or emotional reactions to the experience of searching. Search behaviors can be conceptualized as the building blocks of search roles, as different combinations of search behaviors come together to form the search role profiles. Eight distinct roles exist, but there is overlap in the search behaviors leading to some of the roles. In some cases, it is only the magnitude of a particular search behavior, not its presence, which can determine to which role a participant belongs. For example, many roles are identifiable in part by a participant's verbal discussion while searching. The amount of discussion in which the child is willing to engage can indicate one role over another, as can the topic of a child's speech. We have grouped certain roles together based on such similarities in search behaviors in the following chapters. Overall, there are eight search roles divided into three role groupings: roles of reaction, roles of preference, and roles of proficiency.

Table 2.3: Overview of the Search Role framework

Role Grouping	Search Role	Search Behaviors
Roles of Reaction	Developing	Enthusiastic searches
		Unable to parse complex tasks
		Average level of interface knowledge
	Non-motivated	Lack of interest in search and/or computers
		Limited verbal discussion when searching
		Low level of interface knowledge
	Distracted	Deviation from search task without returning to task
		High level of frustration
		Cannot distinguish advertisements from sought content
		Low level of interface knowledge
Roles of Preference	Rule-bound	Do not deviate from self-imposed search rules
		Verbally discuss school
		Unable to parse complex search tasks
	Domain-specific	Prefer searching in their domain of interest when free to do so
		High level of domain knowledge
		Average level of interface knowledge
	Visual	Prefer to search within images and other media
		Discuss images and other media frequently
Roles of Proficiency	Social	Prefer to search using personal networks or by involving others
		Frequently discuss others in the context of technology use
		High level of source knowledge
	Power	Able to parse complex tasks
		Highly verbal, and verbal about search-related topics in particular
		High level of interface knowledge
		High level of source knowledge

For the 50 longitudinal participants in 2008, there were seven roles: Developing, Distracted, Domain-specific, Non-motivated, Power, Rule-bound, and Visual. In 2013, the same participants showed eight roles; the eighth role of Social Searcher was only observed in participants at older ages (Foss, 2014). Participants most frequently displayed the role of Developing Searcher during both studies, although there were more Developing Searchers during 2008 than during 2013. Ten of the 2008 Developing Searchers moved into the 2013 role of Power Searcher, accounting for all of the growth to the Power role, and there were 13 new Social Searchers in 2013 as well. Domain-specific was also a frequently observed role during both studies, and there were near equal numbers of participants displaying Domain-specific traits across studies. There were also comparable numbers of Visual and Rule-bound Searchers during each year of study. There were slightly more Distracted and Non-motivated Searchers during the 2008 study. As will be discussed in more detail later, the sub-role of Distracted nearly vanished during 2013. The observed role frequencies by study are presented in Figure 2.1.

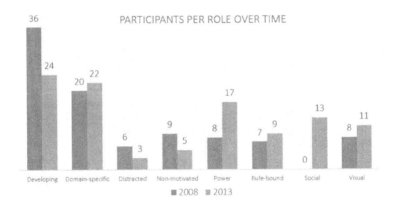

Figure 2.1: Number of participants displaying each search role in 2008 at age 7, 9, or 11 compared to 2013 at ages 10–11, 12–13, and 14–15. 50 total participants, although participants displayed multiple roles.

Some stakeholders may find the gender and age distribution into the roles to be useful information. In general, the roles are not dramatically polarized in terms of gender; most roles had near-equal numbers of female and male participants with the exception of the sub-role of Distracted. The gender information presented in the following figure (Figure 2.2) is aggregated for both the 2008 and 2013 iterations of the longitudinal study, as the overall patterns of role occupancy by gender are fairly similar across the years. There are notable shifts in the roles the participants displayed by age, however, as the age span of children in the studies was from age 7–15. Because of this, the data for role occupancy by age is presented for each age group by study year. Interesting to note are the differences in the percentages of 11-year-olds displaying each role over time; for example, the role of Developing in 2008 had relatively few 11-year-old participants, while in 2013 was mainly comprised of participants aged 10 or 11. When observing these strong shifts, it is important to bear in mind that while there are children aged 11 at both points in time, the studies took place in very different search landscapes, 10-year-old children somewhat distort the data, and there was a more difficult search task added to the interview script in 2013.

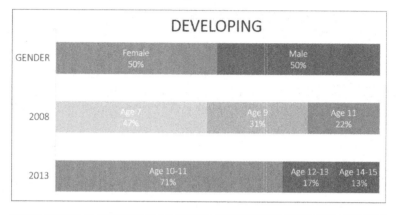

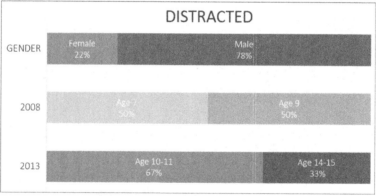

Figure 2.2: Gender and age distribution by role. The top bar shows the percentage of participants in each role who were female or male over the course of the entire longitudinal study. Below this, the percentage of participants in each role from each age is shown, divided by year.

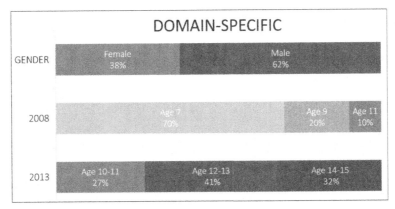

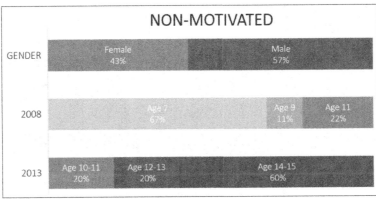

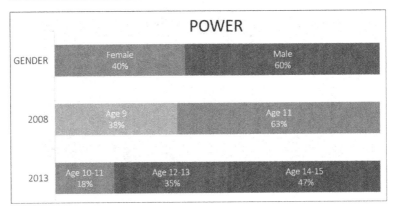

Figure 2.2: Gender and age distribution by role [continued].

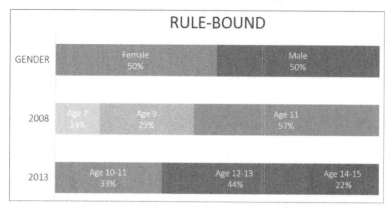

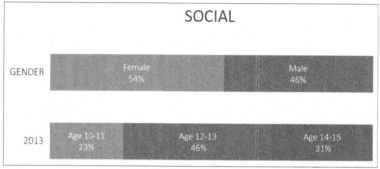

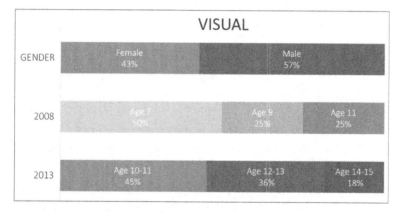

Figure 2.2: Gender and age distribution by role [continued].

Individual participants in both studies frequently showed the traits of multiple roles, as different search tasks completed during the interviews highlighted behaviors specific to different roles (Foss, 2014). For example, when asked to demonstrate a search for their own interest, a participant might display traits of the Domain-specific role, but when completing the complex search task regarding the Vice President's birthday, the same participant could show Power Searcher traits. In these instances, the participants were coded into all applicable roles; one participant could be a Developing, Domain-specific, and Visual Searcher, displaying three search roles. Participants in 2008 displayed between one and four roles per participant. The children in 2013 also displayed between one and four roles per participant. Table 2.4 shows the percentages of study participants in terms of the number of roles displayed. Participants in 2008 were most likely to display only one search role while in 2013 the participants most often displayed two roles. Similar numbers of participants during both studies displayed three roles, and four roles was uncommon, only displayed by three participants in each study.

Table 2.4: Number of roles displayed and percentage of participants by study year		
Number of Roles Displayed	**2008**	**2013**
1	42%	26%
2	34%	46%
3	18%	22%
4	6%	6%

2.3 UPCOMING CHAPTERS

In the remainder of this book, we will rely on the established search role framework to guide our examination of the existing literature. We know from the completed research from the University of Maryland that each role is identifiable by distinct search behaviors, and we seek evidence of these established behaviors within the work of other researchers. Evidence of the search behaviors arising from our own work is omitted from the discussion after the introduction of each search role.

Chapter 3 discusses the roles of Developing, Non-motivated, and the sub-role Distracted. These roles are similar in that children in the roles display stronger emotional reactions to search and show a lower level of interface knowledge. These three roles are referred to as *roles of reaction*. Rule-bound, Domain-specific, and Visual Searchers are grouped in Chapter 4. Searchers in these three roles demonstrate solid preferences and habits for how they engage with search, although they manifest their preferences differently. Identifiable by their habits, these roles are discussed as *roles of preference*. Finally, Power and Social Searchers are discussed in Chapter 5. Children in these roles stand apart mainly in search skill but also in the sophistication of their engagement with search. Power and Social Searchers fall into the *roles of proficiency*. Chapter 6 will provide guidance for stakeholders from the perspective of the role groupings and makes the case for continued research on children's Internet search.

CHAPTER 3

Roles of Reaction: Developing and Non-Motivated Searchers

As searchers, some children can be distinguished from others primarily by their emotional reaction to the experience of searching. Although manifested quite differently in their level of enthusiasm, children in the roles of Developing and Non-motivated have highly noticeable affective responses when seeking information. Developing Searchers are notably enthusiastic when searching, and are eager simply to be using the computer. More negative emotions, ranging from dislike of searching to uncertainty, place a child more firmly into the role of Non-motivated. While this dichotomy of emotions toward search itself is apparent for the roles of Developing and Non-motivated, there are numerous other emotions occurring during searching that do not associate to roles, with the exception of frustration. Frustration with perceived search failure is notably higher for children in the sub-role of Distracted than for children in other roles.

3.1 DEVELOPING SEARCHERS

The image of the elementary-aged child struggling alone to locate information on the Internet is pervasive throughout the literature on children's search. However, what researchers have been less attuned to is the overall positive regard some children have for the Internet and search despite their struggles. A notable characteristic of Developing Searchers is their attitude toward searching, as these children appear willing and excited with search tasks and computer use. Even when challenged with difficult search tasks, Developing Searchers maintain their curiosity. Despite their enthusiasm, they cannot parse complex tasks, which contain many separate concepts, into component pieces. In addition, Developing Searchers display decidedly average search interface knowledge and search skill when compared to children in other roles.

3.1.1 ENTHUSIASM TOWARD SEARCH

Previous literature repeatedly describes children who are eager, willing, and excited to use the Internet. Children may even be eager to engage with search engines, despite the problems they encounter. However, these references to engagement have not been systematically paired with children's search abilities and deficits. Hirsh (1999) described 10-year-old students eagerly collecting information for a class project, jumping into their research immediately. More recent research finds similar trends in attitude. Kammerer and Bohnacker (2012) found that when asked how much they liked searching on the web, three-quarters of their 8- to 10 year-old participants replied positively. Large and Beheshti (2000) observed this highly positive attitude toward the Internet in some of their 12-year-old participants. The authors describe these students as "technophiles" and state, "The technophiles by and large favored the Web in comparison with print sources as a source of information for school projects. They did not necessarily endorse all aspects unreservedly, but overall were 'sold' on the Web" (p. 1072). Borgman et al. (1995) characterized their 9–12-year-old participants as persistent searchers when unsuccessfully searching, while also acknowledging that the observed persistence might have been due to researcher observation.

For older children, Fidel et al. (1999) found that adolescent searchers reported joy from searching on the web despite frustrations; the students found there was a variety of information available and appreciated the availability of images. Davies (2011) described a dichotomy of positive and negative attitudes held by adolescents toward technology in the home environment. Davies attributed positive attitudes to not only strong connections with peers but also to children echoing the attitudes of parents who may work with technology. From a survey of middle and high school teachers, Purcell et al. (2012) described students' willingness to search the Internet, which they attributed to the ease with which students were able to retrieve information as compared to print-based search. This is echoed in Bowler (2010), who reported adolescent's enthusiasm for search even given restrictions of the school setting and the imposed nature of a school assignment.

Other researchers describe a similar positive attitude in combination with reservations. Shenton and Dixon (2003) described the excitement surrounding Internet use in younger participants, but also note that positive attitudes were easily muted when children encountered problems. Shenton and Dixon additionally mentioned that their younger participants relied on parents to ease the difficulties of Internet search, leading to more positive attitudes, while their adolescent participants lacked close parental aid and were often less enthusiastic.

Finally, in consideration of platform, the recent rise in mobile device use and ownership for children has been noted to have a positive impact on attitudes surrounding Internet search. Purcell et al. (2012) discussed that mobile devices in particular can create excitement around learning because students can use their devices to search for information immediately, rather than having to postpone until they are out of class or reach a computer.

3.1.2   INABILITY TO PARSE AND NATURAL LANGUAGE QUERIES

In the past, search interfaces did not adequately support the use of natural language queries. This was detrimental particularly for children, who are more likely than users in other age groups to use phrases or natural language when entering queries (Duarte Torres and Weber, 2011; Nicholas et al., 2011). Past research with children using search engines that did not support the use of natural language found that children were frequently unsuccessful (e.g., Bilal, 2000); keyword query formulation proved to be a major stumbling block for children. Further, when given the choice to interact with a search system via category browsing, keyword entry, advanced search, or by alphabetical list, children overwhelmingly chose to browse a hierarchical taxonomy or alphabetical list (Beheshti et al., 2010). Browsing interactions have been established as reducing cognitive load for children when formulating their information needs, as they can select from limited options rather than recalling keywords from memory (Beheshti et al., 2010; Marchionini, 1989).

Terms entered into a search system even today should ideally reflect an understanding of how information is organized and how the system functions to retrieve results, but children in particular do not possess these deep understandings (van der Sluis and van Dijk, 2010). Children's' more limited vocabulary can cause problems during query formulation (Kafai and Bates, 1997; van der Sluis and van Dijk, 2010) and can cause delays in searching due to needing to reformulate original queries (Duarte Torres et al., 2010).

However, times have changed as have features of search engines. A more recent examination of children using the Google search engine found that natural language queries were not only supported by the interface, but led to better results (Kammerer and Bohnacker, 2012). Despite this evolution search engines, typing a query into a search engine is still not necessarily a single-step operation. Complex search tasks require a searcher to run multiple searches, piecing together information from each search to arrive at a solution. Children have been found to type longer queries than other users. This may be indicative of the complexity of the query entered as well as difficulty the user may be having in formulating the query (Duarte Torres et al., 2010). However, other research has found that longer or natural language queries include more keywords, and therefore can provide results with more comprehensive page titles and answers contained in the snippets of text (Kammerer and Bohnacker, 2012).

3.1.3   AVERAGE KNOWLEDGE OF INTERFACE FEATURES

Search engines contain numerous features designed to aid users with spelling, navigation, or discovery of resources. Developing Searchers display an average level of knowledge of these search interface features when compared to children in other roles. Although children are not always aware of all the features offered by a search system, Solomon (1993) stated that this knowledge grows as users become more familiar with a system and cautions that learning the features can be a daunting task. Druin et al. (2009) described that children aged 7–11 did not use the drop-down spelling assistance even when having spelling difficulty. It was found that children's attention was focused not on the screen, but on their own hands as they struggled to type. Participants under the age of 11 in Solomon's (1993) research with OPACs used system features infrequently, and Hirsh (1999) reported no fifth-grade participants using system features. Marchionini (1989) described an age effect when it came to children choosing to use system features. Older children, around age

12, were much more successful at using system features than were participants around age 10. Bilal (2002) found that 12–13-year-old children did not use the help feature of the search portal Yahooligans!. Overall then, the body of preceding work shows that use of a majority of system features is relatively uncommon for children.

3.2   NON-MOTIVATED SEARCHERS

The popular press might have us believe that every young person is an impassioned computer user, enjoying every moment of Internet immersion. This is not the case. Not all children are interested in computer use, searching, or the potentials of the Internet. Children who seem disengaged with computers and searching while at the same time are tolerant toward the necessity of Internet use fall into the role of Non-motivated Searcher. While generally possessing few search skills, Non-motivated Searchers are highly efficient at searching, often locating information quickly from snippets, or short summaries, on the search engine results page. The strategy of relying on snippets is not the most reliable way to obtain complete and trustworthy information, but it does allow Non-motivated Searchers to bypass steps in the search process that they find to be frustrating. Compared to children in other roles, these searchers do not discuss or indicate awareness of many features of the search engine, especially at age 11 or younger. Additionally, Non-motivated Searchers are extremely limited in how they verbalize their search experience, are not interested in reflecting on their actions, and do not use technology terms.

We have found in our research that the role of Non-motivated is transient. In Foss's (2014) longitudinal study examining the same children at two points in time, Non-motivated Searchers did not remained in the role, instead heavily shifting into the Developing role. This change in Non-motivated Searchers, from being unwilling and disengaged searchers into highly motivated and engaged Developing Searchers, is encouraging, as it indicates that unhelpful attitudes, beliefs, and experiences surrounding search are able to be altered over time.

3.2.1   AMBIVALENCE TOWARD TECHNOLOGY

Van der Sluis and van Dijk (2010) linked interest (engagement) and motivation, stating that children need interest and understanding of a problem in order to become motivated to tackle the challenge via search. In the context of Non-motivated Searchers, the lack of interest and search knowledge leads to a lack motivation to engage with the online search process. This disengagement with technology and searching shown by Non-motivated Searchers is one of their most easily identified characteristics, and other researchers have noted similar affects in searchers of all ages. In a study of preschool children's interactions with the computer, Plowman and Stephen (2005) wrote: "There is a paradox when our observations showed that boredom, frustration, and disengagement were common responses [to the computer] but features associated with play (such as fun, pleasure, spontaneity, and enjoyment) were rarely observable in activities referred to as *playing* with the computer." For older children, Davies (2011) provided a thoughtful discussion regarding the formation of ambivalent attitudes toward technology in a longitudinal examination of the interplay between parental and adolescent attitudes toward technology in the home environment. Davies noted that a reserved attitude toward technology in adolescents seems to be the result of the acceptance of technology wariness or reticence held by parents, the desire to perform well academically (which is perceived as best accomplished via textbooks), or due to attempts to distance themselves from prevailing ways of interacting with peers online.

3.2.2   LIMITED KNOWLEDGE OF INTERFACE FEATURES

Non-motivated Searchers have very few search skills and a notable lack of understanding of features of search engines. As mentioned above, van der Sluis and van Dijk (2010) drew a direct connection for children between poor search skill and poor motivation. In a survey of teachers, Purcell et al. (2012) reported several findings pertaining to a general lack of search skill in students. Teachers in the study relayed that class time was spent to educate students on how search engines function, how to search more effectively, and how to judge the reliability of found information. For many teachers, students were rated as only "fair" or "poor" for the ability to formulate suitable queries and general comprehension of how results are generated. In Bilal's (2000) study, successful searchers were found to possess more knowledge of the functions of interface features than children who were unsuccessful searchers. Use of Boolean operators is reportedly extremely rare for children (e.g., Shenton and Dixon, 2003; Schacter et al.,1998), although in research on early information retrieval systems, Marchionini (1989) did report participants using these features.

3.2.3   LIMITED VOCABULARY AND VERBALIZATION

Using topic-specific language is an indication that a searcher is comfortable and familiar with computers and searching. Familiarity with specific terms regarding computers and search allows children to communicate more directly with peers and adult stakeholders to search regarding their search discoveries, explorations, and questions. In the same way that verbosity and vocabulary knowledge are related to search skill, terseness and limited vocabulary are related to a lack of search skill. Identifying a Non-motivated Searcher is largely accomplished by not only understanding affect, but also by listening to speech (or lack of speech) during search tasks. When discussing searching or the search interface, Non-motivated Searchers use computer or search vocabulary terms at lower rates than children in other roles. Hirsh (1999) described students (especially girls) responding to researcher questions by stating they did not know why they made decisions when retrieving information. Hirsh infered that the lack of ability to articulate searching choices could have an impact on children's ability to determine whether source content is relevant to the information need.

3.3   A ROLE APART: DISTRACTED SEARCHERS

The role of Distracted Searchers almost exclusively co-presents with the role of Non-motivated Searcher. Because of the heavy overlap with another role, the role of Distracted is more of a subtype of Non-motivated Searchers than a distinct role. Distracted Searchers are fairly uncommonly observed, especially in children over the age of 11. The role is nearly extinct for younger adolescents; Distracted Searchers were not observed at all in Foss et al.'s (2013) work with older adolescents, and was the most sparsely populated role shown in children aged 7–15 during Foss (2014). This finding is consistent with Fidel et al. (1999), who discussed that adolescents searching for a school assignment were extremely focused, maintaining their attention on the searching task at hand by using written assignment sheets and referring to them frequently. It is therefore possible that the role of Distracted does not occur frequently enough to warrant detailed future research or separate considerations. This section will introduce what is understood about Distracted Searchers: their patterns of search, their frustration when searching, and their lack of understanding of advertisements.

Causes of distraction for Distracted Searchers are primarily based within the computer, but are not limited only to the computer. Falling into six categories, distractions include: ads on webpages, using the bathroom, engaging with games, events in the physical environment of the search, watching videos, and irrelevant websites (Foss, 2014). For Distracted Searchers in Foss (2014), the most common reason for failing to complete a search task was for all children clicking links to irrelevant websites and for younger children specifically, playing online games.

3.3.1   FOCUS WHEN SEARCHING AND PURPOSEFUL BROWSING

Children may explore unrelated topics while searching by unexpectedly clicking links, entering new queries, or revisiting sites, and this type of deviation from a search goal is not atypical. Children in general have less focus on the search goal and browse more than adult searchers, especially in the early stages of search (van der Sluis and van Dijk, 2010). However, for some children, becoming more directed toward the goal as searching progresses may not occur at all. Other activities seem to interrupt the search process for these children. Distracted Searchers are those who require prompting to remain on or return to the search task that they began and who repeatedly drift away from paths that will lead to their initially sought information. Bilal (2000) and van der Sluis and van Dijk (2010) both observed this tendency, describing children's searching as chaotic. Because children display unpredictable search patterns as a matter of course, it is important to only consider children who are entirely unable to return to the search task at hand to be Distracted Searchers.

In contrast to the casual exploration of links of interest, Borgman et al. (1995) more traditionally described browsing as "an interactive process of skimming over information and selecting choices. Browsing relies on recognition knowledge and requires less well-defined search objectives than does directed keyword searching" (p. 666). Notably, purposeful browsing lessens the cognitive load of search, as children are able to select information of interest from a finite list rather than having to generate keywords from memory (Beheshti et al., 2010; Marchionini, 1989). In contrast, Jochmann-Mannak et al. (2010) found their participants used more search than browse strategies, as did Beheshti et al. (2010) in a query-log analysis for a children's portal offering browsing and keyword search. Schacter et al. (1998) reported that searchers in their study were highly likely to browse, which was measured by visits to different websites.

Despite the frequency of browsing in children, some research has found browsing to be a less effective way for them to locate information. Chen et al. (1998) pointed out that browsing exposes the users to only a very small portion of a dataset. Bilal and Wang (2005) discussed that browsing, while suited for less defined tasks, requires that the searcher has some knowledge of how the sought information will be unearthed from levels of categorization or will be organized. Hirsh (1995) found that children with domain knowledge, or understanding of a particular topic area, were less successful at browsing and were also more likely to browse.

Other research poses the opposite view, holding that browsing can be beneficial for children. For example, Dresang (2005) called for a reevaluation of the assumption that browsing is generally considered to be a less effective search strategy. Large and Beheshti (2000) noted that their participants frequently browsed, defined as undirected exploration of results. In examining how children interacted with a search portal offering keyword search and browse options, children overwhelmingly chose to browse (Beheshti et al., 2010). Chung and Neuman (2007) described high school participants relying on browsing strategies at the early stages of an information-seeking task, as it allowed them to gain a sharper focus for proceeding into the more specific strategy of keyword search.

3.3.2   FRUSTRATION

The affect, or emotional responses, present in a searcher can impact children's information seeking processes. Bilal (2005) discussed that the Internet poses many challenges to children when searching. Not only do children have to develop strong search skills, they also must modulate their emotional reactions to the information seeking process in order to be successful searchers. With older children, Kuhlthau (1991) established a number of emotions connected to phases of the information seeking process. Kuhlthau's participants reported optimism, frustration, and disappointment when searching. Burdick (1996) also reported many of these same emotions in her high school participants.

In adults, Poddar and Ruthven (2010) reported physical reactions to searching in the form of sighs and fingernail-biting. For Large and Beheshti (2000) participants were most frustrated by not finding a few highly relevant sites. Other researchers have reported frustration in adolescents ages 16–18 due to needing to control curiosity during imposed information-seeking tasks, as curiosity can lead to being overwhelmed by the amount of available information (Bowler, 2010).

3.3.3   ADVERTISEMENTS

Distracted Searchers were found to be highly unaware of advertisements, and may experience difficulty in distinguishing when a link will lead to a sponsored website. Valcke et al. (2011) characterized commercial websites aimed at children, such as game sites with available paid content, as risks to children's online safety. They noted that many young children were not able to distinguish commercial from non-commercial sites. Children in Duarte Torres and Weber (2011) confirmed this, as they were more likely to click on ads than adult users. Duarte Torres and Weber make the additional point that increased clicking on ads is indicative of children's confusion, as ads are not generally targeted for young audiences. Eickhoff et al. (2011) described targeting children via commercial websites and child-oriented advertisements as unethical and exploitative of children's inexperience, and note that many websites with appropriate children's content have banner advertisements that render the sites unsuitable for children. It was found that children were likely to report advertisements when asked what they dislike about using the Internet for school assignments (Large et al., 2002, 2004). Livingstone and Bober (2006) additionally listed exposure to commercial content as a risk to children on the Internet. Adolescents in Fidel et al. (1999) were aware of advertisements and reported liking the ability to access both commercial and non-commercial information when searching for school assignments.

CHAPTER 4

Roles of Preference: Rule-Bound, Domain-Specific, and Visual Searchers

Rule-bound, Domain-specific, and Visual Searchers have more apparent differences from each other than similarities, making their grouping somewhat counterintuitive. However, searchers in these three roles are notably more skilled than Non-motivated or Distracted Searchers, and yet lag far behind Power and Social Searchers (see Chapter 5). Rule-bound, Domain-specific, and Visual Searchers are roles largely defined by search preferences; search is restricted by predetermined and self-imposed guidelines, or self-limited to within a topic area, or to information in visual format.

4.1 RULE-BOUND SEARCHERS

When asked the reason for choosing a particular search result over another, a child might respond, "I always pick the first one." This response indicates that the child is relying on pre-existing strategies for search success instead of adapting to the context of the particular search. These preexisting strategies can be called "search rules." Children falling into all roles espouse rules, or guidelines, to explain their search choices and habits. Children also frequently follow their rules shortly after stating them or when engaging in a typical, familiar search. However, continually following an established rule or set of rules despite approaching different types of search tasks and for entire searching sessions is fairly uncommon. Children who display this rigid and repetitive searching are called Rule-bound Searchers. Rules can fall into a number of categories: rules about which websites are safe to use; how to select a result; the format for query composition; and the sequence of events in the search process. Only children who adhere to their own rules, even when the rules are detrimental to the search process, are considered to be Rule-bound Searchers.

Often, the source for search rules is internal; children repeat strategies that have proven to be successful. However, parents and the home setting can also impose rules on children, such as how much time they are allowed on a computer or what type of content is acceptable to explore. Additionally, children are influenced by teachers and other adults in the school setting, with Rule-bound Searchers particularly susceptible to influence. Such common rules include *do not select search results that lead to Wikipedia* and *always choose the first few search results*. Search strategies learned and enforced in school can bleed into search in all contexts, even when a child is free to search without restrictions.

4.1.1   SELF-IMPOSED RULES

In early research investigating children's use of OPAC system, Solomon discussed "ritual moves," or habitual ways children in his study searched (1993, p. 255). Solomon's participants of all ages relied on rules such as pluralizing their search query, typing alternate word forms of the same query, and gauging the query's appropriateness depending on whether searching for an author or subject. Agosto (2002) discussed that self-imposed time constraints were occasionally a limitation for adolescents searching in her study. Davies (2011) found this same unilateral prohibition on Wikipedia, but stemming from parents and teachers rather than from children. Shenton (2007) discussed in depth the rote pattern of Internet searching he has repeatedly observed in participants, calling children's searching formulaic despite the vast resources available to them.

When applied as general guidelines to aid in decisions regarding search, self-imposed search rules can be helpful for child searchers. They can speed the processes of query formulation and result selection, and can serve as bridges spanning points of confusion. For Solomon's participants, (1993) the child searchers' rules sped up the search process as well as allowed young users to lessen the cognitive load required to search.

4.1.2   PARENTAL AND HOME RULES

Parental rules and attitudes regarding their children's use of home computers have a notable impact on the child. Parents of children from age 8–18 with household rules or limitations surrounding their children's use of computers, TV, and other media have children who are more social, less bored, and achieve academically (Rideout et al., 2010). In a study of children's home technology use, Davies (2011) discussed that the majority of parents embrace technology in the home as a way to facilitate their child's learning. Earlier research found that parents regarded the Internet with a degree of wariness, and were more comfortable with their children using CD-ROM resources instead of the Internet (Shenton and Dixon, 2003).

Research has found varying rules imposed by parents on their children's computer use. Parents in Rideout et al. (2010) had two major categories of rules, time and content. Most frequent were time rules, which limited the length of time a child could engage with the television or computer. Content rules restricted the child's access to types of or particular television shows or websites. When describing children entering queries into the Google search engine, Kammerer and Bohnacker (2012) discussed that some of their participants had difficulty with the keyword searching prescribed by parents. These participants asked researchers for approval to search using natural language, expressing relief when discovering they could try this strategy. Parents have also been found to be protective of their children's online identities by checking Facebook profiles or searching for their child's name (Common Sense Media, 2013).

4.1.3   EDUCATOR AND SCHOOL RULES

Search rules imposed in the educational setting also heavily color children as searchers in the home. Fidel et al. (1999) described some adolescent participants completing an assignment in the classroom as allowing the assignment instructions and boundaries to alter their normal searching habits. Chung and Neuman (2007) also discussed participants being heavily influenced by teachers' instructions regarding sources for information, striving to locate relevant and reliable information. Other research suggested that children interacting with search interfaces are highly influenced by their school's expectations, and can take on the predominant search goal of performing highly in response to their school's expectations (Lee et al., 2011), rather than satisfying information needs or searching for exploration. Rules specific to school settings can be found to include: frequent need for time constraints; a need to assign search tasks that meet educational goals; and a requirement that students use credible sources (Bowler, 2010; van der Sluis and van Dijk, 2010). These restrictions affect children's ability to complete searches successfully, learn content retrieved via search, and enjoy the experience of searching (Bowler, 2010; van der Sluis and van Dijk, 2010).

Overall, children and adolescents can change their natural search behaviors to comply with external pressures often imposed from the school setting. Prior research shows influence from school in all aspects of children's search, from reasons to begin searching, selection of results, determining relevancy, and satisfaction from the search experience. It is not necessarily a negative that children are adaptable searchers when given instruction, but if the instruction limits a child's ability to find the information they are searching for or inhibits their engagement in exploring, searching, or learning, then rules can be a detriment.

4.2   DOMAIN-SPECIFIC SEARCHERS

Children often have areas of particular personal interest, and use the Internet as a way to access information about these topics. Domain-specific Searchers gather information via search around a specific topic of interest (e.g., games, horse videos, DeLorean cars). The main characteristic of Domain-specific Searchers is their expert or near expert knowledge pertaining to searching on specific interests. Illustrating a predominant domain for children, Duarte Torres and Weber (2011) report that children search for online games more than for other topics. For children in the role of Domain-specific, domain searching motivates the majority of their computer use. Other traits of children in the role of Domain-specific Searcher include a positive and verbal affect toward their domain, but occasional reticence to search if the task is not about their domain.

Domain-specific Searchers present differently at younger or older ages. Older Domain-specific Searchers are aware of particular websites, but only about a third of searchers age 11 and under in this role discuss specific websites (Foss, 2014). This irregularity in the way the role manifests is explained by the changing nature of domains as children age. When younger, children are more concerned with content categories (e.g., sports) than with the source of the content (e.g., ESPN).

As children grow older, their particular domains generally become more sophisticated and tied to sources. For example, children have been reported to repeatedly visit known websites to keep updated with an area of interest (Shenton and Dixon, 2003). Another age-based difference for Domain-specific Searchers is the broadening of search skills to enable exploration beyond the domain of interest. At age 11 and under, Domain-specific Searchers are not always able to adapt the knowledge gained within their domain to the general searching context. At older ages, however, Domain-specific Searchers are more often observed as co-occupying the highly-skilled role of Power (Foss, 2014). It appears that Domain-specific Searchers over the age of 10 or 11 are able to translate specific skills from their preferred contexts and apply them when searching for more general information.

4.2.1   DOMAIN KNOWLEDGE

Wildemuth (2003) defined domain knowledge as "the searcher's knowledge of the search subject or topic" (p. 247). Children are less likely than adults to rely on domain knowledge when searching, despite the aid this knowledge can provide (van der Sluis and van Dijk, 2010). Children who do possess high domain knowledge have been found to be extremely flexible searchers when searching within their domains (Hirsh, 1996). They are able to employ a number of different approaches to different search tasks, and have a particular ability to refine a search using multiple queries (Hirsh, 1996). Wildemuth notes that domain knowledge is "conceptually distinct from knowledge of searching techniques" (2003, p. 247), and this sentiment was echoed in other research (van der Sluis and van Dijk, 2010). Marchionini (1989) characterized the manifestation of domain knowledge as the ability to formulate appropriate keyword for a given search task; this is a broad definition, as almost all children are able to enter at least one relevant query.

4.2.2   SOURCE KNOWLEDGE

Differing from domain knowledge, which is independent of search, source knowledge refers to the sites with which children are familiar enough to recognize as useful to a task and can easily access. Known sources are often accessed via navigational searches; a user is aware of information existing on a particular website and performs a search for the site's title to aid in navigating to the site or simply enters the URL directly. Knowing sources for information is widely useful; beyond being able to trust an information source or bypass search altogether, children more easily choose a result when they are aware of the URL presented on the search engine results page. Shenton and Dixon (2003) discussed that a knowledge base of sources aids children in avoiding the retrieval of unreliable information. Further, knowledge of sources has been discussed as possibly leading a child to initiating a search or formulating an information need due to the belief that the information will be available (Shenton, 2007).

Related to source knowledge is the action of revisiting already-found websites. Children are often unlikely to deeply evaluate the content they encounter on the Internet, and as a result, they are unlikely to revisit the same website (Nicholas et al., 2011), impairing their ability to build a knowledge base of sources for information. Goldman et al. (2012) reported that undergraduate students classified as better learners and who performed as better searchers revisited websites more often than students who were considered more challenged learners. In contrast to knowing informational websites, children ages 8–12 in Blackwell et al. (2014) identified their favorite gaming and social media sites by name, listing YouTube, Facebook, and Disney as the top three favorite sites. These same children also were able to identify reliable information sources, listing PBS Kids in the top ten favorite sites. Other sources, such as Wikipedia or Kahn Academy, were also mentioned, although with less frequency (Blackwell et al., 2014). An interesting tactic used by adolescents in Chung and Neuman (2007) for retaining information was not to learn websites, but instead to print relevant information as a way to revisit it anytime. Further, adolescents in this study displayed shallow reading of found information; they accepted the possibility of needing to return to a site rather than fully digesting information at the time which it was encountered.

4.3   VISUAL SEARCHERS

Children in all roles conduct intentional image searches, for reasons ranging from wanting to demonstrate their knowledge of the search engine to observers or needing to quickly retrieve a picture for a school assignment. However, *repeatedly* conducting intentional image searches, even when a keyword search might be easier, is much less common. These behaviors indicate a strong preference for information in visual formats, and are unique traits to children belonging to the Visual role. Visual Searchers purposefully choose to locate information within pictures, videos, or other graphical media whenever possible (Druin et al., 2010; Foss, 2014). Visual searching can be accomplished by: using an image search feature in Google or Bing; watching YouTube videos; seeking graphs and charts; or simply ignoring textual information on websites in favor of scanning photos or drawings accompanying the text.

The role of Visual is distinguished further by two factors: definite co-occurrence of other roles and inappropriate application of visual search. First, Visual Searchers always co-occupy other roles; Visual as a role is not seen in isolation. This is because of the necessity to occasionally seek information within text (however much disliked). When demonstrating this more traditional searching, Visual Searchers do not display their visual preference, instead showing other roles. Second, Visual Searchers' preference for non-textual information can occasionally occlude more reasoned or rapid approaches to a particular search task. Although images have the advantage of being briefly scanned for relevance (Slone, 2003), they cannot satisfy all information needs. Similarly, videos are not always appropriate as judging the relevance of video content is difficult without investing quite a bit of time.

4.3.1   VISUAL SEARCH PREFERENCE

Using graphics and other media as information sources during search has been shown to both hinder and aid children. In a comparison of children's searching of computer and print sources, 7-year-old children relied heavily on visual information when searching in an online encyclopedia (Cooper, 2002). This preference did lead to search success, but incurred long delays, demonstrating the choice of visual search as a non-optimal strategy. Another study similarly found images as the causes of search delay (Slone, 2003). Due to their high interest in visual information, participants ages 7–12 were willing to wait for a website to load images, even irrelevant images, before continuing to search. Slone seemed to dismiss the notion that children in this age group could be finding valuable information within the graphics, as she noted that looking at pictures coincides with the recreational goals prompting the participants to search. Contrary findings from Hirsh (1999) discussed 10-year-old participants as highly selective of image content. For example, participants researching athletes preferred individual photos as opposed to a photo including the entire team. Large and Beheshti (2000) found similar results in their study of 12-year-old searchers competing a class research project. In this study, many students searched for visual content to include in their poster presentations. Not only did these participants select images based on relevancy to their topic, but they also were able to successfully employ image search.

In terms of result presentation, visual information cues contained within results pages are conclusively helpful. When tracking the eye movements of children reading a results page, younger participants, those in grades 5 and 7, tended to visually skip around the results page, responding to bolded search terms (Dinet et al., 2010). Other research has also found that graphics can clarify results pages for children, as children ages 8–12 readily made use of clickable images presented as results (Jochmann-Mannak et al., 2010). These findings support the notion of visual cues as being helpful to younger children, especially when selecting results.

Important to note is that children have not universally embraced the utility of non-textual information. Some research has found that children are quite likely to click on pictures at an equal rate as they do text (Gossen et al., 2011). In Large and Beheshti (2000), a faction of students reported that textual information was more important than information conveyed in images. Students in this study additionally were unenthusiastic regarding video and audio content available to them via the Internet. Likewise, Large et al. (1998) reported that children using CD-ROM searching tools did not rely heavily on visual information as a primary source, as they infrequently took advantage of multimedia aspects of their programs, preferring instead to read text.

4.3.2   DISCUSSING NON-TEXTUAL CONTENT

A final identifying characteristic of Visual Searchers is the content of their verbal exchanges regarding search; these children speak of images, video, YouTube, and similar sites at high percentages under the age of 11 and higher percentages than children in other roles at older ages (Foss, 2014).

Visual Searchers may describe watching online videos, searching, copying, and saving images, or explain their visual search process. Other research has noted instances of participants talking about non-textual search. In a study of selection criteria for books in an online library, many participants discussed illustrations as a reason for selecting a particular book (Reuter, 2007). Adolescent students searching in the classroom in Fidel et al. (1999) described relying on website graphics to rapidly judge whether the website was relevant to their needs. The participants talked about deciding whether to engage with website text based on finding the photos not only relevant, but, interesting. Not all children talk easily about visual search; children in Cooper (2002) verbally indicated that they had used pictures in print information sources, but had difficulty explaining why they preferred visual information over text.

CHAPTER 5

Roles of Proficiency: Power and Social Searchers

The roles of Social and Power form a final grouping focused around the high level of search skill displayed by children searching. These two roles overlap heavily, with many children falling into both roles. Social Searchers are less skilled than Power Searchers, although still are notably skilled in their own right. Children in both roles are further distinguished by the amount of verbal discussion in which they engage, although for Power Searchers, the content of the discussion is largely disclosing their search knowledge, and for Social Searchers, the content of the discussion is largely focused on how others triggered or helped with their search experience.

5.1 SOCIAL SEARCHERS

Social search can be thought of as any search-related activity that involves interactions or collaborations with other people (Evans and Chi, 2010). Social Searchers' primary use of computers, devices, and the Internet is for social media or communication with others. While using the computer, they are likely to engage in conversations with other people, whether online or with people in their physical environment. Social Searchers make use of all social aspects when using the computer, for example completing homework assignments with friends using programs such as Skype (http://www.skype.com). They additionally refer to socially searching at a higher rate than adolescents in other roles. Social Searchers freely discuss not only the people influencing their computer use, but are also articulate when describing the ways in which other people affect them. Social Searchers are likely, and much more likely than children in other roles, to report that they are triggered to begin searches due to the influence of other people. Social Searchers were not observed in children under the age of 11 (Foss et al., 2012), but this may not be the case in the current search landscape, as social computer use continues to escalate.

5.1.1 SOCIAL SEARCH AND COMPUTER USE

Morris et al.'s (2010) study with adult Facebook (http://www.facebook.com) and Twitter (http://www.twitter.com) users revealed motivations for seeking answers via social networks over traditional search engines. Social network questioning can allow the asker to phrase questions in natural language and to pose more complicated questions that can be entered as a search query. Additionally, those asking a search question may have more trust in their social networks, and believe that social networks are better resources for recommendations. They may also believe that search engines cannot answer all of their questions. Children, and especially adolescents, also desire a social Internet experience, and searching the Internet socially has the potential to help children improve and develop social skills. Johnson (2012) found that broad uses of the Internet lead to positive social development in children 8–12 years old. Teachers in this study rated children with home Internet access as having more friends than children without Internet access in their homes. Large and Beheshti (2000) pointed out that children in the classroom setting collaborating in groups are less likely to make searching errors, as multiple children are able work together to spot and correct an error. Other research has found that online peer interaction can aid in social identity development (Hannaford, 2012; Livingstone and Bober, 2006). Some search systems, such as in Abbas (2005) have allowed children to share interesting websites and broad search questions with others. However, social or collaborative search and computer use is not currently well-supported, whether within the search interface or among co-located children.

5.1.2   INFLUENCERS TO SEARCH BEHAVIOR

Dresang (2005) found that children had a desire to search on the computer with others and to share their knowledge. This desire to engage socially on the computer, whether searching or not, is a prominent characteristic for Social Searchers. Different groups of people, or influencers, can act as sources of search-related knowledge. For example, search behaviors in children are often influenced by peers, parents, or teachers.

Influencers can be close in age to the child they influence. Peers, friends, siblings or classmates are all sources for search knowledge. Spavold (1990) found that when children ages 9–11 are learning how to navigate an unfamiliar database, they rely heavily on peers whom they perceive to have mastery over the system. This was confirmed by the 11- and 12-year olds in Large et al.'s (1998) study, who cooperated by allowing one child to search while others offered suggestions. Hirsh (1999) also found that children retrieved information for their schoolwork based on what they perceived their peers would find interesting. Fidel et al. (1999) found that adolescents engaged in searching in the school setting were likely to share searching knowledge with each other. Children in Hannaford (2012) with older siblings had broader computer skills, and other research describes children sharing computers with siblings, the reliance very young searchers may develop toward assistance provided by older siblings, or that siblings may prevent or supervise access to computers (Jewitt and Parashart, 2011; Shenton and Dixon, 2003). Kafai and Bates (1997) noted that participants largely had observed siblings using computers.

Parents are also a source of search influence. Hirsh found in her 1999 study set in an elementary school that fifth grade students did not mention parents as influencers, although this could be due to low home Internet penetration rates at the time of the study as well as the school research setting. Davies (2011) discussed that adolescent searchers can adopt the views of their parents toward technology, whether positive or negative. While parents may perceive risks in online communication, children are generally accepting of parental limits and observation to ensure their safety when interacting with others online (Davies, 2011; Madden et al., 2012). Parents in Jewitt and Parashart (2011) were supportive of computer use and sometimes required that children use the computer primarily for schoolwork. For further discussion of parents as influencers, see Chapter 3.

Finally, children are heavily influenced by teachers and other adults at school. Agosto et al. (2012) described that adolescents frequently communicated with their teachers using text or email. Children searching at school for assignments are frequently restricted in the amount of time available for using the computer, the sites they can visit, and are assigned to small research groups by teachers (e.g., Kafai and Bates, 1997; Large et al., 1998; Marchionini, 1989). In some situations, in addition to assigning topics or search tasks and research groups, teachers also dictate the format for how children present retrieved information and stress the use of databases (Chung and Neuman, 2007). Teachers themselves have reported focusing on imparting skills about judging the quality of retrieved information when working with students (Purcell et al., 2012). However, Nesset (2013) reported the interesting finding that the process of search was marginalized by a teacher who was more focused on students being able to make use of found information. As Nesset indicated, search as a specific skill can be unimportant for educators, who are often focused on other aspects of teaching information literacy. For a full discussion of teachers as influencers, also refer to Chapter 3.

5.1.3   SEARCH AND MOBILE DEVICE USE

Social use of devices is clearly important, as children ages 7–12 spend more time using their mobile device to text with other people than engaging in other types of activities, such as listening to music or playing games (Rideout et al., 2010). Agosto et al. (2012) described how adolescents using mobile devices choose their mode of communication with others depending on the depth and urgency of their information needs. Adolescents in the study preferred texting for urgent and minor information needs, but turned to email, Facebook, or telephone calls when freed of time restrictions or when needing in-depth responses.

Beyond this type of device-based information engagement with others, children also use their devices to access information from the Internet. In their study of web site preferences, Blackwell et al. (2014) found that a quarter of the 8–12-year-old participants owned a mobile device such as a smartphone or tablet and that the participants used these devices to access similar content as they would on the computer; while playing games often, the participants also frequented Google, Wikipedia, and educational sites. Purcell et al. (2012) reported that half of the teachers participating in their study allowed students to use their mobile devices to access class-related information during class time.

5.1.4   DISCUSSING SEARCH WITH OTHERS

Social Searchers display the tendency to discuss other people frequently, and also engage others both on and offline while they are searching. Despite using separate computers, adolescents in Fidel et al.'s (1999) research engaged others socially, asking peers in the same room what they had searched for, as did younger children in Large et al. (1998). When searching in small groups, children in 4th and 5th grade determined the next step in their search process by coming to a consensus via voting (Bar-Ilan and Belous, 2007). In order to achieve the consensus, children showed that they were very capable of discussing search with others and weighing the opinions of their peers. When using computers to play games, children will share the experience by watching the screen next to them and by engaging other children in conversation about the gameplay (Sandvig, 2006). Hannaford (2012) found 8- and 9-year-old children eager to join a computer club dedicated to Internet game-playing, describing the popularity of the club growing as children talked about their experience with their peers. Children in Dresang (2005) expressed a desire to share search and computer use experiences with others. Interestingly, half of the children aged 11–16 in Livingstone et al. (2010) reported preferring to interact with others only via the Internet; they did not want company in their physical environment when online.

Not all children are able to collaboratively search. For 7-year-old children working together at a desktop computer, search decisions were not made collaboratively but rather by the child controlling the mouse; the children did not vocalize their opinions about the next step in the search process (Cooper, 2002). Wecker et al. (2010) created a series of scripts to the left side of Google's search screen to prompt 14-year-old learners to collaborate with a partner in the steps relating to finding information via Google. Researchers found that having prompts available to structure collaborative search throughout the entire search project aided students in conducting more successful searches. However, if these scripts were slowly removed over the course of a search project, the students were unable to continue to use the knowledge on conducting strong searches.

5.2   POWER SEARCHERS

Children are often portrayed as naïve users of search interfaces, unable to find information and hampered by adult-oriented systems. However, children that are Power Searchers do exist and this role is much stronger in search skills than other roles. These types of searchers formulate queries using keywords, and are highly verbal and are able to explain their search strategies. Power Searchers type more skillfully and spell queries correctly more often than searchers in other roles. Power Searchers are also confident, stating their intentions prior to clicking or typing and then following through to successfully locating needed information. Children that display the role of Power Searcher also know of sources for information, especially above the age 11. Power Searchers are the only role to use social media or networking sites at age 11 or younger, and are more likely than almost all other roles (except Social Searchers) to frequent such websites at age 11 and above (Foss, 2014).

Most notably, Power Searchers are the only role to appropriately approach complex tasks, as they understand when a particular task requires them to enter more than one query and then assemble a solution. In contrast, children in other roles tend to type long queries with many phrases or unrelated parts when presented with a complex search task, and cannot reach a solution. Children displaying the role of Power are unique among the search roles in the ability to parse complex tasks requiring multiple searches into separate queries (Druin et al., 2010). As Developing Searchers are defined by their inability to parse complex tasks and Power Searchers are defined by their ability to do so, these two roles are mutually exclusive; one searcher is never both a Power and Developing Searcher.

5.2.1   EXPERIENCE EQUALING EXPERTISE

Aula and Nordhausen (2006) provided a review of searching literature focusing on adult users, demonstrating that most existing search research defines expert and novice users based on the number of years they have engaged with search, computers, or the Web. For adults, experience can be measured in years without much difficulty. For children, however, limits on the amount of time they are permitted to use the computer, the frequent sharing of computers with siblings or parents, and the simple fact of their young age all affect the count of years of experience.

Marchionini (1989) based his research on the assumption that young searchers would have less developed mental models of the search systems and tasks, as such models develop over time and with experience. In his study, the older participants, and therefore those with more computer experience, were more successful searchers. Bilal (2000) confirmed the link between experience and expertise in her research with children, finding that children with more search experience were generally more successful searchers. However, Bilal did report that one participant with less than a month of computer experience was a successful searcher and one participant with 6–12 months of experience (a high level) was an unsuccessful searcher. Bilal measured experience in months rather than years as is common for adults: no experience, less than a month, one to three months, and 6–12 months.

Dinet et al. (2010) measured children's prior experience with both the computer and with the Web in their eye-tracking study with participants aged 10–16. The authors found that experience with computers and the Web increased with participant age. Children perceived by their parents as having a higher computer and Internet experience level are less stringently monitored than children with lower levels of experience (Valke et al., 2010). Fidel et al. (1999) explained that the adolescents in their study relied on prior experiences with search to direct their approaches to study tasks.

5.2.2   VOCABULARY AND VERBAL

Child searchers who display frequent use of computer-related vocabulary and the ability to engage in verbal discussion while searching are also likely to be more expert searchers. Power Searchers in particular are likely to correctly name computer and search-related features, as they know many technology vocabulary terms. Slone (2002) analyzed the vocabulary of public library Internet users of all ages when asked to describe the Internet. Slone, who had some participants under the age of 17, reported that library users who employed more sophisticated vocabulary words (e.g., modem, network) were also users of Internet tools, focused in their searching, and knew when to stop searching. See Chapter 3 for more discussion of computer-related terminology. Fidel et al. (1999) described participants as verbally engaged with one another when conducting searches, asking each other for help and dispensing advice regarding search techniques. As Power Searchers are reflective, they are able to provide reasoned justifications for their methods of search. Similarly, in a study comparing the searching of better and worse learners, Goldman et al. (2012) found that undergraduate students who were considered to be better learners were more likely to verbally discuss their choices when searching. By verbally reflecting on their decisions, the participants in Goldman et al.'s study were able to become more aware of the worthiness of the source of information and how to navigate among sources. The increased awareness in turn led to more focused learning and understanding of content. The participants in Large and Beheshti (2000) did not provide much reflection on their browsing, although were verbal about their search experiences.

5.2.3   HIGH KNOWLEDGE OF INTERFACE FEATURES

Prior research shows that children who have knowledge of search interface features are more skilled at searching. Bilal (2000) found that more successful searchers were more aware of more interface features, and that success was additionally reflected in experience. Kafai and Bates (1997) also described a link between prior experience and knowledge of interface features. Students in their study with interface knowledge directed their peers when working in groups regarding selecting websites and were able to evaluate websites for quality, as they determined the length of time the group spent on a particular website. In adolescents, Fidel et al. (1999) described participants successfully making use of navigational system features. More advanced young searchers in Slone (2003) displayed the ability to use advanced search strategies and combinations of approaches to search.

5.2.4   ABILITY TO PARSE

The type of task a user attempts to complete through Internet searching can alter search behavior. Tasks have been characterized on two dimensions: imposed or self-generated (e.g., Gross, 2006; Russell and Grimes, 2007), or simple ranging to complex (e.g., Byström, 2002; Schacter et al., 1998). In adults, Russell and Grimes (2007) discussed differences in search behaviors for imposed and self-generated search tasks. The findings of this study suggested that searchers spend more time and formulate fewer queries on tasks that are self-generated. The authors also explained that browsing might be the cause for these findings; that searchers had few alternate queries for their own tasks and that they spend time browsing due to expecting to recognize the information they are seeking. Gross (1999) pointed out that imposed query search behavior is affected by the relationship between the imposer and the searcher. In 2006, Gross found in her results with imposed queries in adolescents that the students consulted more information sources for imposed tasks than for self-generated tasks.

In looking at task type in terms of complexity, Schacter et al. (1998) examined searching in children ages 11–13, characterizing search tasks in two major categories. *Finding tasks* are challenges that have a definitive answer, while *searching tasks* indicate problems in which the searcher does not know what information will suffice as an answer. The authors found that children performed poorly on the well-defined finding tasks, but were much more successful when searching for the ill-defined searching tasks. They proposed that this could be due to the wide variety of answers available for more complex tasks and that these tasks can be answered through browsing, which children prefer over searching. For adult searchers, Byström (2002) described task complexity as an interaction between a searcher and the task. For example, when a searcher is able to rely on knowledge to formulate a plan for approaching a task, the searcher perceives the task as less complex. Byström found that more complex tasks, those where searchers did not have a planned approach or knowledge, caused searchers to attempt broader strategies to reach an answer, including the consultation of more sources for information. Foss et al. (2012, 2013), in contrast, measured task complexity independently of the knowledge of the participant. Instead, tasks requiring a greater number of queries were regarded as more complex than tasks that could be solved using a single query. For Foss et al., the term "complex search" described search tasks that contained multiple concepts. If entered in natural language, these queries returned no results. Complex tasks could only be solved when separated into independent queries that the search engine can process. Solomon (1993) found that some children in his study of elementary school OPAC users entered multiple concepts as single queries, as did Bilal (2001).

CHAPTER 6

Conclusions

Search roles as we have conceptualized them in this book are a collection of search behaviors distinguishing a habitual or preferred method of Internet search. Search roles are differentiated approaches to search tasks in combination with factors such as affect, social use patterns, skill level, or interest, and become apparent when viewing children's search from a child-centric viewpoint. No one study from previous researchers reports all of these roles for children as searchers. Despite prior studies using different methods, settings, and search technologies, during very different time periods; distinct types of child searchers do arise repeatedly.

6.1 SEARCH ROLE FRAMEWORK AND THE EXISTING RESEARCH

There are eight distinct search roles: Developing, Non-motivated and its sub-role of Distracted, Rule-bound, Domain-specific, Visual, Social, and Power (Druin et al., 2010; Foss, 2014; Foss et al., 2012, 2013). This book has presented the search roles and their predominant traits and uncovered evidence of the roles as existing in the prior literature. Table 6.1 provides a summary of the connections between the search role framework and the existing literature.

Table 6.1: Connections between search role framework and the existing research literture

Grouping	Role	Characteristics	Prior Research
Roles of Reaction	Developing	Enthusiasm toward search	Hirsh, 1999; Kammerer and Bohnacker, 2012; Large and Beheshti, 2000; Fidel et al., 1999; Davies, 2011; Purcell et al., 2012
		Inability to parse complex search tasks	Duarte Torres and Weber, 2011; Bilal, 2000; van der Sluis and van Dijk, 2010; Duarte Torres et al., 2010; Kammerer and Bohnacker, 2012
		Average knowledge of interface features	Solomon, 1993; Marchionini, 1989; Hirsh, 1999

Roles of Reaction [continued]	Non-motivated	Ambivalence toward technology and search	van der Sluis and van Dijk, 2010; Plowman and Stephen, 2005; Davies, 2011
		Low knowledge of interface features	van der Sluis and van Dijk, 2010; Purcell et al., 2012; Bilal, 2000; Shenton and Dixon, 2003; Schacter et al., 1998
		Limited vocabulary and verbalization	Hirsh, 1999
	Sub-role: Distracted	Focused search and browsing	Hirsh, 1995; Dresang, 2005; Large and Beheshti, 2000; Chung and Neuman, 2007; Schacter et al., 1998
		Frustration	Kuhlthau, 1991; Burdick, 1996; Poddar and Ruthven, 2010; Large and Beheshti, 2000; Bowler, 2010
		Advertisements	Valke et al., 2011; Duarte Torres and Weber, 2011; Large et al., 2004
Roles of Preference	Rule-bound	Self-imposed rules	Solomon, 1993; Agosto, 2002; Davies, 2011
		Parental and home rules	Rideout et al., 2010; Davies, 2011; Shenton and Dixon, 2003; Kammerer and Bohnacker, 2012; Common Sense Media, 2013
		Educator and school rules	Fidel et al., 1999; Chung and Neuman, 2007; Lee et al., 2011 Bowler, 2010; van der Sluis and van Dijk, 2010

Roles of Preference [continued]	Domain-specific	Domain knowledge	Hirsh, 1996; van der Sluis and van Dijk, 2010; Wildemuth, 2003; Marchionini, 1989
		Source knowledge	Shenton and Dixon, 2003; Goldman et al., 2012; Chung and Neuman, 2007; Blackwell et al., 2014
	Visual	Visual search preference	Cooper, 2002; Slone, 2003; Large and Beheshti, 2000
		Discussing non-textual content	Reuter, 2007; Fidel et al., 1999; Cooper, 2002
Roles of Proficiency	Social	Social search and computer use	Morris et al., 2010; Large and Beheshti, 2000; Hannaford, 2012; Johnson, 2012
		Influencers	Dresang, 2005; Spavold, 1990; Large et al., 1998 Hirsh, 1999; Hannaford, 2012; Jewitt and Parashart, 2011; Shenton and Dixon, 2003; Davies, 2011; Madden et al., 2012; Agosto et al., 2012
		Mobile device use	Davies, 2011; Madden et al., 2012; Agosto et al., 2012
		Discussing searching with others	Fidel et al., 1999; Large et al., 1998; Bar-Ilan and Belous, 2007; Sandvig, 2006; Hannaford, 2012; Dresang, 2005; Livingstone et al., 2010

		Vocabulary and verbal	Fidel et al., 1999; Goldman et al., 2012; Large and Beheshti, 2000
Roles of Proficiency [continued]	Power	High knowledge of interface features	Bilal, 2000; Kafai and Bates, 1997; Fidel et al., 1999; Slone, 2003
		Ability to parse complex search tasks	Solomon, 1993; Bilal, 2001; Schacter et al., 1998; Gross, 2006

6.2   GUIDANCE FOR ADULT STAKEHOLDERS

As described in Chapter 1, this book approaches children's search from a child-centric perspective. This perspective is achieved by thinking of search as an entire experience rather than as comprised of pass or fail steps. Many of the recommendations contained in the previous chapters are useful to practitioners from a detailed standpoint that considers how to support children only at critical points in their searching, and exclude the adjoining and concurrent search processes that may complicate a search. For example, a practitioner may identify a searcher as following a detrimental self-imposed rule to use only recognized sources, leaving the searcher blind to novel information. While the insight into self-imposed rules is useful, focusing only on this aspect of the child's search overlooks strengths the child may have; knowledge of sources is actually a great aid to young searchers. It is difficult to take into consideration the myriad of factors affecting a single search, and the role groupings prove useful in providing boundaries to search problems and avenues for search strength.

The search role framework can be applied by adult stakeholders interacting with children as they search or who are working with search session data originating from children. Identifying children as belonging to a particular role or role group is appropriate for any number of goals: developing search skills; encouraging independent use of the Internet to locate information; simplifying and streamlining the design of search tools and systems; or determining when to intervene and when to allow a child to evolve as a searcher naturally.

6.2.1   PARENTS

Parents are not perpetual influencers, having the majority of their impact on younger children rather than adolescents (Foss, 2014). However, children are aware of the computer and search habits and attitudes of their parents (Davies, 2011), and minor interventions have long-lasting effects (Foss, 2014). Children are also largely accepting of limitations placed on their computer use by parents (Madden et al., 2012). Parents are therefore in a position to impart search skills with no great effort by modeling useful search strategies and making rules.

Roles of Reaction

As Developing Searchers are readily engaged with search, one of the most helpful actions a parent could take is to support their skill acquisition by simply allowing free time for exploration. Children are able to learn much about search when exploring for their own interests, and often are limited in unstructured computer time.

Parents are uniquely able to observe what frustrations arise in their children during searching. As contextual frustration is displayed by children in the less-skilled sub-role of Distracted in particular, aiding children to overcome their frustrations is important. Additionally, in children age 11 and younger in Foss (2014), search interruptions such as connectivity, outdated software, uninstalled plugins, or pop-up ads were major sources of frustration. With routine computer maintenance, such frustrations are entirely avoidable. Parents can prevent negative reactions to the computer in their younger children by performing periodic checks and upkeep of family computers.

For children who are either unskilled or disinterested with the computer, such as Non-motivated Searchers, parents can leverage real-world hobbies and interests to draw children into using the computer. Parents can introduce image search to children interested in visual content, allow children who play instruments or sing to explore music videos on the website YouTube, or encourage children to use social media to communicate with their friends.

The unstructured and safe home environment is particularly suited for encouraging children in all roles, and especially less-verbal Non-motivated Searchers, to talk about technology and searching. Parents can use search and computer-related vocabulary when talking with their children to develop familiarity and comfort with terminology.

Roles of Preference

Household search and computer use rules were not always in alignment with the rules in place in the classroom setting. In the case of Rule-bound Searchers in particular, heavy exposure to school rules created unhelpful search rituals. Coordinating house rules with rules taught at school could provide consistent messages for children learning searching skills and provide a balance between restrictions on computer use at school and the freer access in the home. Parents could communicate with their child's school to determine what the information literacy educator is planning on sharing with their child regarding search, and reinforce the same search concepts. Alternately, parents could teach their children compromises to school rules.

Domain expertise useful for young searchers, as it makes children more flexible and is likely to translate directly into search skill over time (Foss, 2014; Hirsh, 1996). In the home environment, children have the luxury of free time to pursue their own interests through searching on the computer, and in doing so, to cultivate domain knowledge. Parents can leverage real-world hobbies and interests to draw children into using the computer by introducing image search to children interested in visual content, allowing children who play instruments or sing to explore music videos on the website YouTube, or encouraging children to use social media to communicate with their friends.

Roles of Proficiency

The role of Social Searcher is a highly skilled role, and social computer use is frequently connected with positive traits in children (Foss, 2014; Hannaford, 2012; Johnson, 2012). As children displaying social behaviors often also display the role of Power Searcher; encouraging social computer use would likely be beneficial for young searchers. To break down the social wall prohibiting the flow of search information on a peer-to-peer level, parents could support children in the sharing of skills and strategies by encouraging in-person computer co-use among siblings and friends; demonstrate how to use video, voice, and text chat systems; or permit their children's use of email, depending on parent's comfort levels.

6.2.2   EDUCATORS

Although it is tempting to embrace the search strategies of Power Searchers and attempt to impart all searchers with similar skills via education, Aula and Nordhausen (2006) cautioned against precisely this action, stating that search in itself does not draw interest. Instead of training all searchers to become experts, search engines should adapt to the needs of the user. Aula and Nordhausen described as an example the utility of related search and query suggestion features over teaching users to formulate alternate queries.

Roles of Reaction

Developing Searchers are limited largely by their inability to break apart complex search tasks. Explicit teaching of this specific aspect of search skill would likely enable many Developing Searchers to become vastly more effective in their search experiences.

Prior research has suggested that having an adult sit with a young software user to provide aid during exploration of the software. The term "guided interaction" was originally applied only to interface-based assistance, but was extended to include ways in which adults can actively engage children while they use the computer (Plowman and Stephen, 2005). This concept is easily expanded further to apply to aiding child searchers. The suggestions for adult helpers include: explanations of the interface, help with mousing, demonstration of search engine features, sharing enjoyment, rectifying errors, and providing positive feedback. For Non-motivated Searchers in particular, this in-depth assistance could spark engagement and alleviate some of the lack of knowledge of search engines.

Given the differing engagements of Non-motivated and Developing Searchers toward search, perhaps pairing children with computer enthusiasm with those who are more reticent would be a supportive educational experience. In this way, perhaps the positive affect of a Developing Searcher could translate to a Non-motivated Searcher.

Roles of Preference

Despite the fact that children search at home far more than at school, school is a frequently reported reason to begin searching by children in all roles and across all ages. As completing assignments drives children to search, adequate support regarding how to search should be provided by adults in the educational setting. Google provides useful search instruction on their Search Education webpage (www.google.com/insidesearch/searcheducation), and this resource could be implemented in a classroom. Google Search Education provides lesson plans and live training in video form. Video lessons would be especially engaging for Visual Searchers.

For Rule-bound Searchers, more adaptable strategies would be favorable over rigid rules; with rigidity, rules can hinder more than aid children. While the domain name of a site may be important to note, children should also be aware of other indicators of quality websites. Instead of rules regarding perfect query formulation, children should be encouraged to enter many variations on the same query. When presented with numerous results, rules enabling children to differentiate between sites or to change the ordering of the results based on the search task would alleviate some of the challenge of the search engine results page.

The participating children in Foss (2014) demonstrated an increased awareness of video content. Much educational information is available on the Internet in video format, including online education sources such as Udacity, Coursera (http://www.coursera.org) or Khan Academy (http://www.khanacademy.org), how-to videos from sites such as Instructables (http://www.instructables.com) or the variety of videos available from YouTube. Awareness of visual information could be extremely advantageous to children who want to use the Internet as a tool for learning. Educators could promote awareness of sites such as these as well as incorporate visual tools into coursework to aid children in learning new strategies that coincide with their search preferences. Using video content would support Visual Searchers as well as increase domain knowledge for children in all roles, which is desirable when helping children to build search skill.

Roles of Proficiency

Complex search questions involve a lack of one-to-one correspondence between the search task and the search queries required to answer them; complex tasks require that children have the skills to break complex tasks into component parts. To teach these skills, search can be presented as a step-by-step process that involves dynamic generation of a search plan based on initial query results, as opposed to a fixed process of query entry followed by result selection. In the classroom, information literacy educators can encourage trial and error within the search interface rather than formulaic strategies to build adaptable skills in children.

Google Search Education, in addition to providing video tutorials, hosts the A Google a Day (http://www.agoogleaday.com) search challenge. This daily question poses difficult and variously approached search tasks, requiring extensive knowledge of features of the search engine Google as well as general knowledge. Power Searchers could expand their ability to use search engine features through solving A Google a Day.

Children during the longitudinal interviews demonstrated their habits of keeping their mobile devices close at hand, checking notifications from friends or news apps, and in some cases, receiving phone calls and texts during the short time span of the interviews. Mobile devices are owned at high rates (Common Sense Media, 2013), and were highly integrated with daily life as reported by children and their parents in Foss (2014). Using the already-familiar routine of interacting with a mobile device can provide a way to informally spread search knowledge, especially when attempting to connect with Social Searchers. Texts from educators or educational systems that contained search tips, hints, or challenges, or the development of a mobile application devoted to search literacy could reach children via their devices, easing the in-class burden of teaching search skill.

6.2.3   DESIGNERS

There are numerous opportunities for designers of search tools when considering the search role framework. The information regarding search skill acquisition through social means, increased social computer use, recurring frustrations, strategies more skilled children develop, and effects of the changing search landscape all pose actionable areas for development. Designers can implement change to search systems that directly support search competency in children without requiring the children to adapt to the interface. Although researchers have proposed and created separate search interfaces designed to be used only by children, children prefer to use the same interfaces that are used by adults (Jochmann-Mannak et al., 2010).

In the past, it has been a common practice to attempt to solve user search problems by adding interface features with specific functions. As an example, young searchers (and often all searchers) experience difficulty spelling. To alleviate this problem, search engines tools have been added that enable the user multiple ways to progress successfully with a search without knowing how to correctly spell a query. These search tools include dropdown menus below containing clickable search terms, automatically corrected result retrieval, and indicators at the top of the results pages showing the correctly spelled term. However, young searchers experience a wide range of difficulties and strengths, and these differ for each individual. Therefore, addressing the needs of child searchers by the addition of features to the search interface may not be optimal. It is likely that for a given individual, unnecessary features will be included and needed features will be missing. While researchers have designed child-friendly search interfaces based on the recommendations of the existing literature, when these systems were evaluated, children demonstrated their wide-ranging needs and skills, some of which were missing in the system (Gossen et al., 2012; Jochmann-Mannak et al., 2010).

Roles of Reaction

Identifying children who differ from their peers along the dimension of positive or negative regard toward search is fairly straightforward with the opportunity to observe individual children searching. More difficult, however, is the problem of identifying these children from datasets of search actions. Given this, reliance on emotion as a flag for belonging to a role is best for adult stakeholders who have direct contact with children as they search.

Large et al. (2002) found that most of their most participants liked the idea of including games within search portals, describing the games as having the potential to provide entertainment and increase enjoyment during research. Other research has defined the suitability of websites for use by children by including factors such as interactivity and appeal (Gyllstrom and Moens, 2010b). Given Non-motivated Searcher's disengagement with computers and search, it is possible that games or other perceived fun interactive elements within search engines could draw interest.

Google's Voice Search (http://www.google.com/insidesearch/features/voicesearch), a feature allowing users to speak their queries, could potentially eliminate frustration for children with limited interface knowledge, such as children in the roles of reaction. Voice search is readily available on mobile handheld devices, although for families with older home computers, this feature is not always accessible due to the requirement of integrated or functional microphones.

Designers of search tools could help children in roles of reaction by attempting to duplicate or scaffold the successful skills demonstrated by Power Searchers. Power Searchers seem to be aware of sources before searching. Presenting websites with diverse content as highly ranked results, as opposed to websites useful to only specific search scenarios, can help to establish known sources. Additionally, an interface designed to support building a knowledge base of sources might allow users to choose to see already viewed sites higher on the results page to establish site familiarity. Power Searchers have the ability to break apart complex search tasks into separate queries. Children in the role of Developing in particular often struggle with this skill, entering complex tasks in natural language. A search engine tool suggesting a step-by-step search that is triggered by the appearance of a lengthy or natural language query could support the development of parsing skill. Wecker et al. (2010) established work in this area by providing prompts to searchers within the context of an ongoing search.

Less adept children frequently focus their gaze on their hands when typing search queries, as locating the correct keys is not yet a rote behavior. Given that their focus is not on the screen, children therefore do not always see the helpful interface features such as the autocomplete menu. By adding subtle audio cues when such features are activated, children could be encouraged to shift their attention to on-screen features. In addition, the bottom of the screen real estate should be well-used to attract children's attention away from their typing on the keyboard.

Roles of Preference

The related or similar searches feature of many search engines' results pages can reduce query entry to a click and alleviate query formulation difficulties as well as allow children a new way to explore their domain of interest. Simply repositioning the related terms feature within the search engine results page could encourage more awareness and use. In their research into a method for presenting reading-level appropriate results pages, Collins-Thompson et al. (2011) suggested allowing the interface to teach critical vocabulary for searched-for topics if the user does not enter the vocabulary as search terms (Collins-Thompson et al., 2011). For children in the role of Domain-specific, this could be an additional way to promote domain exploration.

Rule-bound Searchers largely inherit search rules from teachers, and these rules are taught without contingencies for different search scenarios. Given that Rule-bound Searchers are willing to internalize rules from external sources, there is an opportunity for the search interface itself to propose rules and appropriate exceptions to the rules. Interfaces could provide explanations for why some results are presented as more relevant on the results page to clarify rules surrounding which result ranks are best to click.

Eickhoff et al. (2011) discussed that visual content existing within a website may be used as a way to classify the site as one that is more child-friendly, as young children find visual information easier to process than text.

Van der Sluis and van Dijk (2010) explained that motivation to search based on domain interests is a key factor to bear in mind when creating search systems that are designed for children. Providing searchers with resources such as related websites or different queries that integrate neatly into existing domain knowledge is one way to leverage motivation (Chen et al., 1998; van der Sluis and van Dijk, 2010).

As children in roles of preference demonstrate decidedly different approaches to search, search engines could support children by offering multiple ways to search. For example, searchers could begin by clicking on a letter of the alphabet to access lists of keywords, by browsing subject categories, or by using the existing keyword and natural language search box (Large et al., 2002; Rocha Silva and Xexeo, 2013). Additionally, Solomon (1993) discussed the importance of displaying the relationships between subject headings visually.

Various researchers have presented arguments for including visual results for children. Fidel et al. (1999) pointed out that in addition to providing added criteria for selecting relevant results, images or graphical cues contained within results are much faster to scan than reading text. For Fidel et al., this type of visual cue would be most appropriate when large numbers of results are presented. Gossen et al. (2012) discussed that including images as category clues to website content may be a way to assist young children with limited reading ability. When examining children's interface preferences, Large et al. (2002) found that children not only appreciated graphical and colorful design elements, but also were engaged with characters acting as search interface guides or representatives. Gyllstrom and Moens (2010a) lamented the lack of visual cues and graphical results on search engine results pages for children, specifically pointing out the opportunity to include coloring pictures, mazes, puzzles, maps, music, and other interactive learning materials. Van der Sluis and Van Dijk (2010) provided a discussion of how to approach search systems to support children. The authors note that methods of querying a system and for the system to present results can be altered to provide young searchers with alternate and visually-based ways of querying and perceiving search results. Azzopardi et al. (2012) also pointed out that video searching and browsing interfaces can be a way to allow very young children to engage with media safely as well as avoid difficult keyword-input interfaces.

Roles of Proficiency

Based on the desire children have for social and collaborative computer use, designers could develop search tools that make other people more accessible as resources. For example, Moraveji et al. (2011) developed a classroom tool called ClassSearch for teaching and learning the successful search strategies of others. The system displays queries and websites visited on a large screen at the front of the classroom. The instructor then easily points out successful queries and sources to the class for discussion. Motivated by ClassSearch, Bederson et al. (2012) developed SearchParty. This is a collaborative search system intended for classroom use, allowing students to see the queries of classmates. Systems such as this would support social computer use for children in all roles, and would be especially suited for supporting Social Searchers.

Integrating search with social networks would not only support the current behavior of children, but also draw children into search concurrently with seeking social connectivity. Research conducted in this area includes work exploring how to integrate Web 2.0 features such as the bookmarks or tags of others into one's search results (Amitay et al., 2009) and increasing relevance of documents based on social media status updates or whether people the searcher knows have interacted with the documents (Karweg et al., 2011).

The activities children report engaging in with others via the Internet span two major dimensions: synchronous versus asynchronous, and co-located versus remote. Children discuss the synchronous activity of chatting with others as well as the asynchronous use of email. Children also report co-located device sharing, such as passing a phone back and forth. This is in contrast to remotely connecting with friends to play online video games. Systems designed for collaboration among multiple users should take into account the breadth of ways children report interacting with others. Children and adolescents clearly desire unrestricted types of interaction within a system.

6.3   NEED FOR CONTINUED RESEARCH

6.3.1   CHANGING SEARCH LANDSCAPE

It is undeniable that the search landscape shifts dramatically every few years. Attention is focused on users' engagement with closed datasets, creating models of the information seeking process, whether searching or browsing interfaces are most appropriate, emotional factors affecting search, effects of different types of tasks, or the use of search tools on mobile devices, all depending on the evolving and advancing technology used in searching. Research and theories regarding children's responses to the changing search landscape tend to lag behind those for adults. Researchers have been stymied by attempting to understand children's information seeking as it occurs on adult-oriented interfaces and with largely adult-oriented datasets, or with beginning their research from philosophies attributing search deficit to children. Search for children will likely never be considered a "solved problem."

There is a need to continue to ensure that research into how children search is updated as the larger context of search changes. Searches that are considered challenging in the current search landscape do not always remain challenging. As an example, Foss (2014) used the complex task, "Which day of the week will the Vice President's birthday be on next year?" This task was quickly outdated as search engines not only provided the query in the autocomplete, but also linked directly to the answer (see Figure 6.1). This question will likely be difficult for only the short time frame following the 2016 presidential election before again being answered by avid research participants.

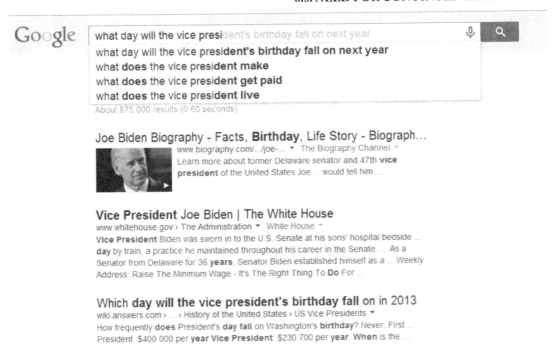

Figure 6.1: Example of the changing search landscape from June, 2014. Children from Druin et al. (2010) contributed content to question-answering sites, rendering the complex search task "Which day of the week will the current Vice President's birthday be on next year?" much easier for future participants to accomplish. Participants no longer needed to parse the search task, but could enter their query in natural language and use autocomplete as well as click directly on the third result.

In the more distant past, children searched most frequently in schools and libraries. Considerations as to the setting of the search are becoming more essential to understanding how to best design for and educate children and adolescents about search. Prior research has found that children are most likely to go on the Internet in their homes (Rideout et al., 2010). The home environment is technology-rich and offers many alternate activities to computer use (see Figure 6.2 as an example). Children often need adult regulation to access information content from their homes (Livingstone and Helsper, 2008), and this regulation differs from the regulation of schools and libraries as well as across homes, as different parents enforce different rules regarding search and children's use of technology. A main motivation for conducting research in the homes of participants is to gain a clearer understanding of the problems, skills, and typical behaviors children display when searching in the most naturalistic setting possible. By being in the home, researchers can more clearly understand the interplay of factors affecting a young searcher.

Figure 6.2: An example home environment of search from Foss (2014). Siblings' computers in close proximity with headphones and mice, which in this case are preferred over the laptop touchpad. There are numerous alternate activities to the use of the computer in this room alone: a television, video games, movies, books, a bed for napping, and toys. The family also has a large and friendly dog (not pictured) who engages with the siblings frequently.

6.3.2   OBSERVING SOCIAL BEHAVIORS

Social interactions facilitated by social media or applications on mobile devices are vitally important to many children and adolescents, and these interactions may be connected to search behaviors in a number of ways. To clearly observe the social nature of computer use in children and how it related to search, researchers should be aware that methods other than the in-context interview should be used. The interaction between the researcher and the participant during interviews inhibits social activity such as checking Facebook, responding to Skype messages, interacting via email, or watching YouTube videos through a friend's account. Participants may be too polite to engage with social activities during the interview, or may refrain from doing so to protect their private interactions with others from the researcher's scrutiny. Other methods could be used to observe these behaviors; perhaps asking children to log their computer and device use with a video diary would more readily show aspects of social behavior that cannot be captured during a one-on-one interview. Additionally, social information can be obtained via interviews with parents, siblings, and friends of the children, or interviewing more than one participant simultaneously.

6.3.3   RESEARCH INTO MOBILE SEARCH

There is currently a shift away from the use of more traditional technologies, such as desktop or laptop computers, in favor of mobile devices such as smartphones and tablets (Common Sense Media, 2013). Children are increasingly owners of mobile devices (Common Sense Media, 2013), and often share devices with family members (Lenhart et al., 2010). As a result, children and adolescents now have the ability to search from anywhere and at the moment of information need. Children's use of mobile devices for search represents a changing and under-researched area.

Increasing rates of device use by children opens new avenues for search interfaces. Using the camera functions included in devices, children can take photos and perform searches based on those photos (Yeh et al., 2005). This type of searching is particularly useful for locating images from the Internet of similar objects and for searching related to the physical environment, which is no longer constrained to a desk.

The research of Druin et al. (2010) and Foss (2014) spanned an unstable period of time: in 2008, few children owned or even used mobile devices, and so search on devices was not even considered by the authors. By 2013, devices had risen dramatically in prominence for young children, and eight participants chose to use their device during their second interview. Had the first study taken place even a year later, the authors might have uncovered a different picture of children's search: for example, the role of Social may appear in children younger than age 10–11, the youngest age displaying the role as currently established. As a final trend from the 2013 interviews, use of mobile devices seems to negatively impact search skill and increase the likelihood of being a Social Searcher. Eight participants used a mobile device, including iPads, smartphones running iOS, Android, or Windows OS, or Android tablets. Six of the eight children displayed the less-skilled role of Developing Searcher, and four of these six were also Social Searchers. Possibly, these participants rely on their social networks for information, and have less of a need than children on laptop or desktop computers to develop search skills, but such questions will be answered in future research.

Acknowledgments

First and foremost, we thank all of the children and parents who were kind enough to welcome us into their homes during the course of our research studies. Their patience and honesty led to research findings we could not have imagined. This work would not have been possible without support from two important people: Google's Dan Russell whose curiosity and questions challenged us in important ways and Google's Hilary Hutchinson who provided insight and wisdom throughout the years of data collection, analysis, and writing, offering her perspective with lightning-speed emails. We also want to acknowledge the combined efforts and good work of many researchers over the years who helped us to develop the search role framework; Evan Golub, Leshell Hatley, Luis Sanchez, Robin Brewer, Jason Yip, Phillip Lo, Whitney Ford, Mona Leigh Guha, Sonia Franckel, Emily Rhodes, Panagis Papadatos, Chelsea Hordatt, and Leyla Nooroz all devoted their time and expertise throughout the process. Finally, this research would not have been possible without years of generous support from Google Faculty Research Awards.

References

Abbas, J. (2005). Out of the mouths of middle school children: I. Developing user-defined controlled vocabularies for subject access in a digital library. *Journal of the American Society for Information Science and Technology*, 56, 1512–1524.

Agosto, D. E. (2002). Bounded rationality and satisficing in young people's web-based decision making. *Journal of the American Society for Information Science and Technology*, 53, 16–27. DOI: 10.1002/asi.10024.

Agosto, D. E., Abbas, J., and Naughton, R. (2012). Relationships and social rules: Teens social network and other ICT selection practices. *Journal of the American Society for Information Science and Technology*, 63, 1108–1124.

American Library Association. (1989). Presidential committee on information literacy: Final report. http://www.ala.org/acrl/publications/whitepapers/presidential.

American Library Association. (2000). Information literacy competency standards for higher education. Retrieved from: http://www.ala.org/acrl/standards/informationliteracycompetency.

Amitay, E., Carmel, D., Har'El, N., Ofek-Koifman, S., Soffer, A., Yogev, S., and Golbandi, N. (2009). Social search and discovery using a unified approach. *Proceedings of the 20th ACM Conference on Hypertext and Hypermedia* (HT '09), 199–208. DOI: 10.1145/1557914.1557950.

Anick, P., and Kantamneni, R. G. (2008). A longitudinal study of real-time search assistance adoption. *Proceedings of the 31st Annual International ACM SIGIR Conference on Research and Development in Information Retrieval* (SIGIR'08), 701–702. DOI: 10.1145/1390334.1390459.

Aula, A., and Nordhausen, K. (2006). Modeling successful performance in web searching. *Journal of the American Society for Information Science and Technology*, 57, 1678–1693.

Azzopardi, L., Dowie, D., and Marshall, K. A. (2012). YooSee: A video browsing application for young children. *Proceedings of the 35th international ACM SIGIR conference on Research and development in information retrieval*, 1017.

Bar-Ilan, J., and Belous, Y. (2007). Kids as architects of web directories: An exploratory study. *Journal of the American Society for Information Science and Technology*, 58(6), 895–907.

80 REFERENCES

Barsky, E., and Bar-Ilan, J. (2012). The impact of task phrasing on the choice of search keywords and on the search process and success. *Journal of the American Society for Information Science and Technology*, 63, 1987–2005.

Bateman, S., Teevan, J., and White, R. W. (2012). The search dashboard: How reflection and comparison impact search behavior. *Proceedings of the ACM Conference on Human Factors in Computing Systems*, 1785–1794.

Bawden, D., and Robinson, L. (2002). *Promoting literacy in a digital age: approaches to training for digital literacy.* Learned Publishing, 15, 297–301.

Bederson, B. B., Quinn, A. J., and Rose, A. (2012). SearchParty: Learning to search in a web-based classroom. Educational Interfaces, Software, and Technology (EIST), Special Issue in *Personal and Ubiquitous Computing Journal*. Retrieved from https://sites.google.com/site/eist2012/home/program.

Beheshti, J., Large, A., and Tam, M. (2010). Transaction logs and search patterns on a children's portal. *The Canadian Journal of Library and Information Science*, 34(4), 391–402.

Bilal, D. (2000). Children's use of the Yahooligans! web search engine: I. Cognitive, physical, and affective behaviors on fact-based search tasks. *Journal of the American Society for Information Science*, 51, 646–665. DOI: 10.1002/(SICI)1097-4571(2000)51:7<646::AID-ASI7>3.0.CO;2-A.

Bilal, D. (2001). Children's use of the Yahooligans! web search engine. II. Cognitive and physical behaviors on research tasks. *Journal of the American Society for Information Science and Technology*, 52, 118–136. DOI: 10.1002/1097-4571(2000)9999:9999<::AID-ASI1038>3.0.CO;2-R.

Bilal, D. (2002). Children's use of the Yahooligans! web search engine. III. Cognitive and physical behaviors on fully self-generated search tasks. *Journal of the American Society for Information Science and Technology*, 53, 1170–1183. DOI: 10.1002/asi.10145.

Bilal, D. (2005). Children's information seeking and the design of digital interfaces in the affective paradigm. *Library Trends,* 54, 197–208. DOI: 10.1353/lib.2006.0013.

Bilal, D. and Wang, P. (2005). Children's conceptual structures of science categories and the design of web directories. *Journal of the American Society for Information Science and Technology*, 56, 1303–1313.

Bilal, D. (2012). Ranking, relevance judgment, and precision of information retrieval on children's queries: Evaluation of Google, Yahoo!, Bing, Yahoo! Kids, and Ask Kids. *Journal of the American Society for Information Science and Technology*, 63(9), 1879–1896. DOI: 10.1002/asi.22675.

Blackwell, C. K., Lauricella, A. R., Conway, A., and Wartella, E. (2014). Children and the Internet: Developmental implications of web site preferences of 8–12-year-old children. *Journal of Broadcasting and Electronic Media*, 58(1), 1–20. DOI: 10.1080/08838151.2013.875022.

Borgman, C. L., Hirsh, S. G., Walter, V. A., and Gallagher, A. L. (1995). Children's searching behavior on browsing and keyword online catalogues: The science library catalogue project. *Journal of the American Society for Information Science*, 46, 663–684.

Bowler, L. (2010). The self-regulation of curiosity and interest during the information search process in adolescent students. *Journal of the American Society for Information Science and Technology*, 61, 1332–1344. DOI: 10.1002/asi.21334.

Burdick, T. A. (1996). Success and diversity in information seeking: Gender and the information search styles model. *School Library Media Quarterly*, 25(1), 19–26.

Burgstahler, S. (2011). Universal Design: Implications for computing education. *ACM Transactions on Computing Education*, 11(3), Article 19. DOI: 10.1145/2037276.2037283.

Byström, K. (2002). Information and information sources in tasks of varying complexity. *Journal of the American Society for Information Science and Technology*, 53, 581–591. DOI: 10.1002/asi.10064.

Chen, H., Chung, Y.-M., Ramsey, M. and Yang, C. C. (1998). A smart itsy bitsy spider for the web. *Journal of the American Society for Information Science*, 49(7), 604–618.

Chung, J. S., and Neuman, D. (2007). High school students' information seeking and use for class projects. *Journal of the American Society for Information Science and Technology*, 58, 1503–1517.

Collins-Thompson, K., Bennett, P. N., White, R., de la Chica, S., and Sontag, D. (2011). Personalizing web search results by reading level. *20th ACM Conference on Information and Knowledge Management*, 403–412.

Common Sense Media. (2013). Zero to eight: Children's media use in America 2013. *A Common Sense Media Research Study*. Retrieved from: https://www.commonsensemedia.org/research/zero-to-eight-childrens-media-use-in-america-2013.

Cooper, L. Z. (2002). A case study of information seeking behavior of 7-year-old children in a semistructured situation. *Journal of the American Society for Information Science and Technology*, 53(11), 904–922.

Davies, C. (2011). Digitally strategic: how young people respond to parental views about the use of technology for learning in the home. *Journal of Computer Assisted Learning*, 52, 324–335. DOI: 10.1111/j.1365-2729.2011.00427.x.

Dinet, J., Christian Bastien, J. M., and Kitajima, M. (2010). What, where, and how are young people looking for in a search engine results page? Impact of typographical cues and prior domain knowledge. *Proceedings of IHM '10*, 105–112.

Dresang, E.T. (2005). The information-seeking behavior with youth in the digital environment. *Library Trends*, 54, 178–196. DOI: 10.1353/lib.2006.0015.

Druin, A. (2005). What children can teach us: Developing digital libraries for children. *Library Quarterly*, 75(1), 20–41.

Druin, A., Foss, E., Hatley, L., Golub, E., Guha, M. L., Fails, J., and Hutchinson, H. (2009). How children search the Internet with keyword interfaces. *Proceedings from the 9th International Conference on Interaction Design and Children* (IDC '09, 89–96. DOI: 10.1145/1551788.1551804.

Druin, A., Foss, E., Hutchinson, H., Golub, E., and Hatley, L. (2010). Children's roles using keyword search interfaces at home. *Proceedings from the 28th International Conference on Human Factors in Computing Systems* (CHI '10), 413–422. DOI: 10.1145/1753326.1753388.

Duarte Torres, S., Hiemstra, D., and Serdyukov, P. (2010). Query log analysis in the context of information retrieval for children. *Proceedings from the 33rd International ACM SIGIR Conference on Research and Development in Information Retrieval* (SIGIR '10), 847–848. DOI: 10.1145/1835449.1835646.

Duarte Torres, S., and Weber, I. (2011). What and how children search on the web. *20th ACM Conference on Information and Knowledge Management*, 393–402.

Eickhoff, C., Serdyukov, P., and de Vries, A. (2011). A combined topical/non-topical approach to identifying websites for children. *4th ACM International Conference on Web Search and Data Mining*, 505–514.

Eickhoff, C., Serdyukov, P., and de Vries, A. (2012). Supporting children's web search in school environments. *Proceedings of Information Interaction in Context*, 129–137.

Evans, B. M., and Chi, E. H. (2010). An elaborated model of social search. *Information Processing and Management*, 46, 656–678.

Eynon, R., and Malberg, L.-E. (2011). A typology of young people's Internet use: Implications for education. *Computers and Education*, 56, 585–595.

Fidel, R., Davies, R. K., Douglass, M. H., Holder, J. K., Hopkins, C. J., Kushner, E. J.,…Toney, C. D. (1999). A visit to the information mall: Web searching behavior of high school students. *Journal of the American Society for Information Science*, 50, 24–37.

Foss, E., Druin, A., Brewer, R., Lo, P., Sanchez, L., Golub, E., and Hutchinson, H. (2012). Children's search roles at home: Implications for designers, researchers, educators, and parents.

Journal of the American Society for Information Science and Technology, 63, 558–573. DOI: 10.1002/asi.21700.

Foss, E., Druin, A., Yip, J., Ford, W., Golub, E., and Hutchinson, H. (2013). Adolescent search roles. *Journal of the American Society for Information Science and Technology*, 64, 173–189. DOI: 10.1002/asi.22809.

Foss, E. (2014). Internet searching in children and adolescents: A longitudinal framework of search roles. Dissertation.

Gossen, T., Low, T., and Nürnberger, A. (2011). What are the real differences of children's and adults' web search? *Proceedings of the 34th International ACM SIGIR Conference on Research and Development in Information Retrieval* (SIGIR '11), 1115–1116. DOI: 10.1145/2009916.2010076.

Gossen, T., Nitsche, M., and Nürnberger, A. (2012). Knowledge journey: A web search interface for young users. *Proceedings of the Symposium on Human-Computer Interaction and Information Retrieval* (HCIR '12), Article 1. DOI: 10.1145/2391224.2391225.

Goldman, S. R., Braasch, J. L. G., Wiley, J., Graesser, A. C., and Brodowinska, K. (2012). Comprehending and learning from Internet sources: *Processing patterns of better and poorer learners. Reading Research Quarterly*, 47(4), 356–381.

Gross, M. (1999). Imposed versus self-generated questions: Implications for reference practice. *Reference and User Services Quarterly*, 39(1), 53–61. Retrieved from http://www.jstor.org/stable/20863675.

Gross, M. (2006). *Studying children's questions: Imposed and self-generated information seeking at school.* Lanham, MD: Scarecrow Press, Inc.

Gyllstrom, K., and Moens, M. (2010a). A picture is worth a thousand search results: Finding child-oriented multimedia results with collAge. *Proceedings of the 33rd International ACM SIGIR Conference on Research and Development in Information Retrieval* (SIGIR '10), 731–732). DOI: 10.1145/1835449.1835588.

Gyllstrom, K., and Moens, M. (2010b). Wisdom of the ages: Toward delivering the children's web with the link-based AgeRank algorithm. *Proceedings of the 19th ACM Conference on Knowledge and Information Management,*

Hannaford, J. (2012). Imaginative interaction with Internet games. *Literacy*, 46 (1), 25–32.

Hirsh, S. G. (1995). The effect of domain knowledge on elementary school children's search behavior on an information retrieval system: The science library catalogue. *Proceedings of ACM Conference on Human Factors in Computing Systems Doctoral Consortium*, 55–56.

Hirsh, S. G. (1996). The effect of domain knowledge on elementary school children's information retrieval behavior on an automated library catalogue. Dissertation.

Hirsh, S. G. (1999). Children's relevance criteria and information seeking on electronic resources. *Journal of the American Society for Information Science*, 50, 1265–1283.

Hourcade, J. P., Bederson, B., Druin, A., and Guimbretiere, F. (2004). Differences in pointing task performance between preschool children and adults using mice. *ACM Transactions on Computer-Human Interaction*, 11(4), 357–386.

Hughes-Hassell, S., and Agosto, D. E. (2007). Modeling the everyday-life information needs of urban teenagers. In M. K. Chelton and C. Cool (Eds.), *Youth information-seeking behavior II: Context, theories, models, and issues* (27–61). Lanham, Maryland: Scarecrow Press, Inc.

Hutchinson, H. B., Druin, A., and Bederson, B. (2007). Supporting elementary-aged children's searching and browsing: Design and evaluation using the international children's digital library. *Journal of the American Society for Information Science and Technology*, 58(11), 1618–1630.

Jackson, L. A., von Eye, A., Biocca, F. A., Barbatsis, G., Zhao, Y. and Fitzgerald, H. E. (2006). Does home Internet use influence the academic performance of low-income children? *Developmental Psychology*, 42(3), 429–435.

Jewitt, C., and Parashart, U. (2011). Technology and learning at home: Findings from the evaluation of the HomeAcess Programme pilot. *Journal of Computer Assisted Learning*, 27, 303–313.

Jochmann-Mannak, H., Huibers, T., Lentz, L., and Sanders, T. (2010). Children searching information on the Internet: Performance on children's interfaces compared to Google. *Workshop on Accessible Search Systems from the 33rd International Conference on Research and Development in Information Retrieval* (SIGIR '10), 27–35.

Jochmann-Mannak, H., Lentz, L., Huibers, T., and Sanders, T. (2014). How interface design and search strategy influence children's search performance and evaluation. In D. Yannacopoulos, P. Manolitzas, N. Matsatsinis, & E. Grigoroudis (Eds.), Evaluating Websites and Web Services: Interdisciplinary Perspectives on User Satisfaction (pp. 241-287). Hershey, PA: IGI Global. DOI: 10.4018/978-1-4666-5129-6.ch014.

Johnson, G. M. (2012). Internet use and child development: The techno-microsystem. *Australian Journal of Educational and Developmental Psychology*, 10, 32–43.

Kafai, Y., and Bates, M. A. (1997). Internet web-searching instruction in the elementary classroom: Building a foundation for information literacy. *School Library Media Quarterly*, 25(2), 103–111.

Kammerer, Y. and Bohnacker, M. (2012). Children's web search with Google: The effectiveness of natural language queries. *Proceedings from the 12th International Conference on Interaction Design and Children* (IDC '12), 184–187. DOI: 10.1145/2307096.2307121.

Karweg, B., Huetter, C., and Böhm, K. (2011). Evolving social search based on bookmarks and status messages from social networks. *Proceedings of the 20th ACM International Conference on Information and Knowledge Management* (CKIM '11), 1825–1834. DOI: 10.1145/2063576.2063839.

Kolikant, Y. B.-D. (2010). Digital natives, better learners? Students' beliefs about how the Internet influenced their ability to learn. *Computers in Human Behavior*, 26(6), 1384–1391. DOI: 10.1016/j.chb.2010.04.012.

Koltay, T. (2011). The media and the literacies: media literacy, information literacy, digital literacy. *Media, Culture, and Society* 33(2), 211–221.

Kuhlthau, C. C. (1991). Inside the search process: Information seeking from the user's perspective. *Journal of the American Society for Information Science*, 42, 361–371. DOI: 10.1002/(SICI)1097-4571(199106)42:5<361::AID-ASI6>3.0.CO;2-#.

Kuhlthau, C. C. (1993). A principle of uncertainty for information seeking. *Journal of Documentation*, 49, 339–355. DOI: 10.1108/eb026918.

Kuiper, E., Volman, M., and Terwel, J. (2005). The web as an information resource in K-12 education: Strategies for supporting students in searching and processing information. *Review of Educational Research*, 75, 285–328.

Lampe, C., Vitak, J., Gray, R., and Ellison, N. (2012). Perceptions of Facebook's value as an information source. *Proceedings from the SIGCHI Conference on Human Factors in Computing Systems* (CHI '12), 3195–3204. DOI: 10.1145/2207676.2208739.

Large, A., and Beheshti, J. (2000). The web as a classroom resource: Reactions from the users. *Journal of the American Society for Information Science and Technology*, 51, 1069–1080.

Large, A., Beheshti, J., and Breuleux, A. (1998). Information seeking in a multimedia environment by primary school students. *Library and Information Science Research*, 20, 343–376. DOI: 10.1016/S0740-8188(98)90027-5.

Large, A., Beheshti, J., and Rahman, T. (2002). Gender differences in collaborative web searching behavior: An elementary school study. *Information Processing and Management*, 38, 427–443. DOI: 10.1016/S0306-4573(01)00034-6.

Large, A., Beheshti, J., Nesset, V., and Bowler, L. (2004). Designing web portals in intergenerational teams: Two prototype portals for elementary school students. *Journal of the American Society for Information Science and Technology*, 55, 1140–1154.

LeCompte, M. D., and Preissle, J. (1993). *Ethnography and qualitative design in educational research* (2nd ed.). San Diego, California, USA: Academic Press, Inc.

Lee, S. W., Tsai, C.-C., Wu, Y.-T., Tsai, M.-J., Liu, T.-C., Hwang F.-K.,... and Chang, C.-Y. (2011) Internet-based Science Learning: A review of journal publications. *International Journal of Science Education*, 33(14), 1893–1925.

Lenhart, A., Ling, R., Campbell, S., and Purcell, K. (2010). Teens and mobile phones. Pew Internet and American Life Project. Retrieved from http://pewinternet.org/Reports/2010/Teens-and-Mobile-Phones.aspx.

Livingstone, S., and Bober, M. (2006). Regulating the Internet at home: Contrasting the perspectives of children and parents. In Buckingham, D. and Willett, R. (Eds.). *Digital generations: children, young people and new media*. Mahwah, N.J.: Lawrence Erlbaum, p. 93–113.

Livingstone, S., and Helsper, E. (2008). Parental mediation and children's Internet use. *Journal of Broadcasting and Electronic Media*, 52(4), 581–599. DOI: 10.1080/08838150802437396.

Livingstone, S., Haddon, L., Görzig, A., and Ólafsson, K. (2010). Risks and safety for children on the internet: The UK report. LSE, London: EU Kids Online. Retrieved from: http://eprints.lse.ac.uk/33730/1/EU_Kids_Online_Report_Risks_and_safety_for_children_on_the_internet_2010.pdf.

Mackey, T. P., and Jacobson, T. E. (2011). Reframing information literacy as metaliteracy. *College and Research Libraries*, 62–78.

Madden, A. D., Cortesi, S., Gasser, U., Lenhart, A., and Duggan, M. (2012). Parents, teens, and online privacy. Pew Research Center's Internet and American Life Project. http://pewinternet.org/Reports/2012/Teens-and-Privacy.aspx.

Marchionini, G. (1989). Information seeking strategies of novices using a full-text electronic encyclopedia. *Journal of the American Society of Information Science*, 40, 54–66.

Marchionini, G. (2006). Exploratory search: From finding to understanding. *Communications of the ACM*, 49(4), 41–46.

Menard, S. (2002). *Longitudinal research* (2nd ed.). Series: Quantitative applications in the social sciences. Thousand Oaks, CA: Sage Publications.

Moraveji, N., Morris, M. R., Morris, D., Czerwinski, M., and Riche, N. (2011). ClassSearch: Facilitating the development of web search skills through social learning. *Proceedings of the Annual Conference on Human Factors in Computing Systems* (CHI '11), 1797–1806. DOI: 10.1145/1978942.1979203.

Morris, M. R., Teevan, J., and Panovich, K. (2010). What do people ask their social networks, and why? A survey study of status messages and Q&A behavior. *Proceedings from the 28th*

International Conference on Human Factors in Computing Systems (CHI '10), 1739–1748. DOI: 10.1145/1753326.1753587.

Nahl, D. (2004). Measuring the affective information environment of web searchers. *Proceedings of the American Society for Information Science and Technology*, 41, 191–197. DOI: 10.1002/ meet.1450410122.

Nardi, B. (ed). (1996). *Context and consciousness: Activity theory and Human-computer Interaction.* USA: MIT Press.

Nesset, V. (2013). Two representations of the research process: The preparing, searching, and using (PSU) and the beginning, acting and telling (BAT) models. *Library and Information Science Research*, 35, 97–106.

Nicholas, D., Rowlands, I., Clark, D., and Williams, P. (2011). Google generation II: Web behavior experiments with the BBC. *Aslib Proceedings: New Information Perspectives*, 63(1), 28–45.

Plowman, L, and Stephen, C. (2005). Children, play, and computers in pre-school education. *British Journal of Educational Technology*, 36, 145–157.

Poddar, A., and Ruthven, I. (2010). The emotional impact of search tasks. *Proceedings from the 3rd Symposium on Information Interaction in Context*, 35–44. DOI: 10.1145/1840784.1840792.

Purcell, K., Rainie, L., Heaps, A., Buchanan, J., Friedrich, L., Jacklin, A. …Zickuhr, K. (2012). How teens do research in the digital world. Pew Research Center's Internet and American Life Project. Retrieved from http://pewinternet.org/Reports/2012/Student-Research.

QSR International. (2013). QSR International Pty Ltd (Version 10). Retrieved from http://www. qsrinternational.com/.

Rideout, V. J., Foehr, U. G., and Roberts, D. F. (2010). *Generation M2: Media in the lives of 8–18 year olds. A Kaiser Family Foundation Study.* Menlo Park, CA: Henry J. Kaiser Family Foundation. Retrieved from http://www.kff.org/entmedia/upload/8010.pdf.

Reuter, K. (2007). Assessing aesthetic relevance: Children's book selection in a digital library. *Journal of the American Society for Information Science and Technology*, 58(12), 1745–1763.

Rocha Silva, S. R., and Xexeo, G. B. (2013). Child search framework: a collaborative information retrieval architecture to assist children in the search process. *Proceedings of the 2013 IEEE 17th International Conference on Computer Supported Cooperative Work in Design*, 551–556.

Rowlands, I., Nicholas, D., Williams, P., Fieldhouse, M., Gunter, B., Withey, R.,…Tenopir, C. (2008). The Google generation: The information behaviour of the researcher of the future. *Aslib Proceedings: New Information Perspectives*, 60(4): 290–310.

Russell, D. M., and Grimes, C. (2007). Assigned and self-chosen tasks are not the same in web search. *Proceedings of the 40th Annual International Conference on Systems and Software* (HICSS '07), 85–92. DOI: 10.1109/HICSS.2007.91.

Saldaña, J. (2003). *Longitudinal qualitative research: Analyzing change through time.* Blue Ridge Summit, PA: AltaMira Press.

Sandvig, C. (2006). The internet at play: Child users of public Internet connections. *Journal of Computer-Mediated Communication*, 11, 932–956.

Schacter, J., Chung, G. K. W. K, Dorr, A. (1998). Children's Internet searching on complex problems: Performance and process analyses. *Journal of the American Society for Information Science*, 49, 840–849. DOI: 10.1002/(SICI)1097-4571(199807)49:9<840::AID-ASI9>3.0.CO;2-D.

Selwyn, N., Potter, J., and Cranmer, S. (2009). Primary pupils' use of information and communication technologies at school and home. *British Journal of Educational Technology*, 40, 919–932.

Shenton, A.K. (2007). The paradoxical world of young people's information behavior. *School Libraries Worldwide*, 13(2), 1–17.

Shenton, A. K. (2008). Use of school resource center-based computers in leisure time by teenage pupils. *Journal of Librarianship and Information Science*, 40(2), 123–137.

Shenton, A. K., and Dixon, P. (2003). A comparison of youngsters' use of CD-ROM and the Internet as information resources. *Journal of the American Society for Information Science*, 54, 1029–1049.

Singer, G., Pruulmann-Vengerfeldt, P., Norbisrath, U., and Lewandowski, D. (2012). The relationship between Internet user type and user performance when carrying out simple vs. complex tasks. *First Monday*, 17(6), June 4, 2012.

Slone, D. J. (2002). The influence of mental models and goals on search patterns during web interaction. *Journal of the American Society for Information Science and Technology*, 53(13), 1152–1169.

Slone, D. J. (2003). Internet search approaches: The influence of age, search goals, and experience. *Library and Information Science Research*, 25, 403–418. DOI: 10.1016/S0740-8188(03)00051-3.

Solomon, P. (1993). Children's information retrieval behavior: A case analysis of an OPAC. *Journal of the American Society for Information Science*, 44, 245–264.

Spavold, J. (1990). The child as naïve user: A study of database use with young children. *International Journal of Man-Machine Studies*, 32(6), 603–625. DOI: 10.1016/S0020-7373(05)80103-8.

Strauss, A. L., and Corbin, J. (1998). *Basics of qualitative research: Techniques and procedures for developing grounded theory* (2rd ed.). Thousand Oaks, CA: Sage Publications.

Todd, R. J. (2003). Adolescents of the information age: Patterns of information seeking and use, and implications for information professionals. *School Libraries Worldwide*, 9(2), 27–46.

Valcke, M., Bonte, S., de Wever, B., and Rots, I. (2010). Internet parenting styles and the impact on Internet use of primary school children. *Computers and Education*, 55, 454–464.

Valcke, M., de Wever, B., van Keer, H., and Schellens, T. (2011). Long-term study of safe Internet use of young children. *Computers and Education*, 57, 1292–1305.

Van der Sluis, F., and van Dijk, B. (2010). A closer look a children's information retrieval usage. Toward child-centered relevance. *Toward Accessible Search Systems: Workshop of the 33rd Annual ACM SIGIR Conference on Research and Development in Information Retrieval, Workshop*, 3–10.

Wecker, C., Kollar, I., Fischer, F., and Prechtl, H. (2010). Fostering online search competence and domain-specific knowledge in inquiry classrooms: Effects of continuous and fading collaboration scripts. *Proceedings from the 9th International Conference of the Learning Sciences* (ICLS '10), Volume 1, 810–817. Retrieved from http://dl.acm.org/citation.cfm?id=1854464.

Wildemuth, B.M. (2003). The effects of domain knowledge on search tactic formulation. *Journal of the American Society for Information Science and Technology*, 55(3), 246–258.

Wilson, M. (2012). *Search User Interface Design*. Synthesis Lectures on Information Concepts, Retrieval, and Services. Morgan Claypool.

Yeh, T., Grauman, K., Tollmar, K., Darrell, T. (2005). A picture is worth a thousand words: Image based object search on a mobile platform. *Proceedings of ACM Conference on Human Factors in Computing Systems*, 1–4.

Author Biographies

Allison Druin is Chief Futurist for the University of Maryland's Division of Research and is a Professor in the iSchool as well as a researcher in the Human-Computer Interaction Lab. As the University's first Chief Futurist, she works with faculty throughout campus on research strategic planning and partnership development. In her own research over the last 20 years, she has led design teams of children, computer scientists, educators, and more to develop new educational technologies with co-design methods for children. Her research focus has been to understand how children can search, access, use, and create information by developing new technologies. Her team has created a variety of new technologies which have included new mobile storytelling devices, digital libraries to support cultural tolerance, and robotic toys for active learning. Her co-design team has partnered with numerous organizations over the years, including the U.S. National Park Service, UNICEF, National Geographic, and Nickelodeon (where they won an Emmy for their shared design, "the do not touch" button).

When she is not leading research, for the last seven years Druin has been a monthly technology radio correspondent on the local DC National Public Radio Station, WAMU (88.5). On the Kojo Nnamdi Show's Tech Tuesday she discusses the latest tech trends. Druin received a B.F.A in Graphic Design from Rhode Island School of Design in 1985. She then went on to complete a Master's Degree from the MIT Media Lab in 1987, and was awarded her Ph.D. in 1997 from the University of New Mexico.

Elizabeth Foss is a graduate of the University of Maryland, College Park. As a Ph.D. student, she conducted research in the areas of youth Internet search and designed technology with children in the Human-Computer Interaction Lab and College of Information Studies at UMD.

Foss' dissertation research focused longitudinally on how youth, ages 7–15, search the Internet. Starting in 2008, and revisiting the same participants in 2013, she conducted field interviews with youths who demonstrated their Internet search habits. The goal of this research was for educators, technology designers, parents, and researchers to use the search role framework to better support youths as searchers and to encourage better searching habits.

Foss also worked with an intergenerational design team in the HCIL, called Kidsteam, which used Cooperative Inquiry methods to create new technologies, and improve existing ones, for children by working directly with children throughout the entire design process.

Printed in the United States
by Baker & Taylor Publisher Services